Thomas Hardy

Selected Poems

Edited by
WALFORD DAVIES
Director of Extra-Mural Studies,
University College of Wales, Aberystwyth

Dent: London, Melbourne and Toronto
EVERYMAN'S LIBRARY

© Selection, introduction and notes, J. M. Dent & Sons Ltd, 1982

All rights reserved
Phototypeset in 10/11pt Meridien Roman by
D. P. Media Limited, Hitchin, Hertfordshire
Printed and bound in Great Britain by
Richard Clay (The Chaucer Press) Ltd
Bungay, Suffolk
for
J. M. Dent & Sons Ltd
Aldine House, 33 Welbeck Street, London W1M 8LX
First published in Everyman Paperback, 1982

British Library Cataloguing in Publication Data

Hardy, Thomas, 1840–1928
    Thomas Hardy: selected poems.
    I. Title   II. Davies, Walford
    821'.8   PR4742

    ISBN 0–460–11783–1 Pbk

Contents

II *Nature's Look and Evidences*

III   *Men, Women, Places*

IV   *Tales Told*

V *Presences*

VI   *Selves Unseeing*

VII   *Missing Dates*

VIII   *Your Great Going*

Biographical Outline

1839 22 Dec. – marriage of parents: Thomas Hardy (self-employed mason, later bricklayer and master-mason) and Jemima Hand (cook and maidservant); they settle, with Thomas's widowed mother, at Higher Bockhampton in Stinsford parish, near Dorchester.

1840 2 June – Thomas Hardy, eldest child, born.

1841 Mary Hardy (sister) born.

1848 Autumn – first school at Stinsford (the 'Mellstock' of the novels and poems); given Virgil's *Aeneid* and Johnson's *Rasselas* by his mother.

1850 Enters school (British and Foreign Schools Society – Nonconformist) in Dorchester.

1851 Henry Hardy (brother) born. Tryphena Sparks (first cousin) born.

1856 Kate Hardy (sister) born. July – starts apprenticeship under John Hicks, Dorchester architect, working on church restorations. Learns Greek. William Barnes, the poet, ran a school next door.

1857 Meets Horace Moule, early friend and mentor. Grandmother (b. 1772) dies.

1862 Moves to London, to Arthur Blomfield's architectural practice, as draughtsman in church design and restoration.

1863 April – wins prize for architectural design, and silver medal for essay set by the Council of the R.I.B.A. Begins to change mind about permanent career as architect, as also about career in the Church.

1865 18 March – 'How I Built Myself a House' published in *Chambers's Journal*. Buys editions of poetry, histories and manuals of English literature, Nuttall's *Standard Pronouncing Dictionary* and Walker's *Rhyming Dictionary*. Attends Shakespeare performances at Drury

Lane. 1865/7 the period of earliest surviving verse, all unpublished at the time. Oct. 1865/March 1866 – studies French in evening classes at King's College. Inquires about matriculation at Cambridge.

1867 July – returns to Bockhampton as assistant to John Hicks at Dorchester. Aug. 1867/June 1868 – writes *The Poor Man and the Lady* (first novel, later destroyed).

1869 March – meets George Meredith (author of *Modern Love*) who, as publisher's reader for *The Poor Man and the Lady*, advised against publication. June – moves to Weymouth as assistant to G. R. Crickmay, the architect now in charge of the Dorchester firm. Tryphena Sparks had been teaching at Coryates, near Weymouth, since 1868: the summer of a love relationship with Tryphena (H. gave her a ring) and of a return to poetry after failure of first novel. Sept. – starts writing new novel, *Desperate Remedies*.

1870 Jan. – Tryphena enters a London teacher-training college. H. returns to Bockhampton. 7 March – leaves for two-day visit for survey (for restoration) of St Juliot's church, nr. Boscastle, north Cornwall. The rector's sister-in-law, Emma Lavinia Gifford, later became H.'s first wife. May – returns to London, doing some casual architectural work, seeing Horace Moule but not Tryphena, and corresponding with Emma Gifford. Aug. – goes to Cornwall: events and impressions in Emma's company during this summer later celebrated in some of the best poems.

1871 March – DESPERATE REMEDIES published anonymously: mixed reviews, making abandonment of architecture for literature difficult. May/June – in Cornwall, supervising work on St Juliot's church; during this summer writes the novel *Under the Greenwood Tree*.

1872 March – back in London, attached to the architect Thomas Roger Smith. June – UNDER THE GREENWOOD TREE published anonymously. July – offered serial

publication for novel which became *A Pair of Blue Eyes*.
Sept. – returns to Bockhampton, finally abandoning
architectural career. Dec. – invited by Leslie Stephen
to contribute next novel, *Far From the Madding Crowd*,
for serial publication in the *Cornhill* magazine;
Stephen's friendship and critical authority as editor an
important influence.

1873 May – A PAIR OF BLUE EYES published. 21 Sept. – Horace
Moule commits suicide in Cambridge.

1874 17 Sept. – marries Emma Gifford at St Peter's Church,
Paddington; honeymoon in Rouen and Paris, return-
ing to live in London. Nov. – FAR FROM THE MADDING
CROWD published, his first real success.

1875 July – serialization of the novel *The Hand of Ethelberta*
starts in the *Cornhill*. Aug. – the Hardys move to Swan-
age, Dorset. Nov. – the first poem to be published ('The
Bride-Night Fire', in *The Gentleman's Magazine*).

1876 Early March – the Hardys move from Swanage to
Yeovil, Somerset. April – THE HAND OF ETHELBERTA pub-
lished. May/June – a fortnight's tour of Holland and
the Rhine, and Belgium (to visit the field of Waterloo).
July – they move to Sturminster Newton, north-east
Dorset: H. later referred to this period as 'Our happiest
time'.

1877 Jan. – begins writing the novel *The Return of the Native*.
June – makes notes towards 'grand drama' on
Napoleonic Wars.

1878 Jan. – serialization of *The Return of the Native* starts in
the magazine *Belgravia*. March – move to London. Nov.
– THE RETURN OF THE NATIVE published, badly reviewed.

1879 Jan./Feb. – plans the novel *The Trumpet-Major* (serial-
ized throughout 1880 in *Good Words*). Regular
theatre-going, prompting earliest of many plans for
theatrical adaptations of his own work. At this period
meets leading writers like Arnold, Browning, Tenny-
son, Henry James. Edmund Gosse remained a close

friend and literary adviser. H. often ill (internal bleeding) and depressed. July/Aug. – holiday tour in Normandy.

1880 Oct. – THE TRUMPET-MAJOR published, very well received though not a financial success. Oct. 1880/May 1881 – writes *A Laodicean*, mostly dictated to Emma because of illness; the novel commissioned, for serialization later in 1881, by *Harper's Magazine*.

1881 June – move to Wimborne, Dorset. Plans the novel *Two on a Tower*. Aug./Sept. – tour of Scotland. Dec. – A LAODICEAN published.

1882 May/Dec. – *Two on a Tower* serialized in the *Atlantic Monthly*. Autumn – they spend several weeks in Paris. Late Oct. – TWO ON A TOWER published, badly received.

1883 Winter – move to Dorchester; building started of their final home, Max Gate (designed by H., built by his brother Henry).

1884 Starts writing the novel *The Mayor of Casterbridge*. April – elected J.P. for Borough of Dorchester.

1885 June – they move into Max Gate. Nov. – starts writing the novel *The Woodlanders*.

1886 May – THE MAYOR OF CASTERBRIDGE published, well received. 7 Oct. – William Barnes dies. Reading at British Museum for *The Dynasts*.

1887 March – holiday in Italy. THE WOODLANDERS published.

1888 May – THE WITHERED ARM (collection of short stories) published. June/July – in Paris. Autumn – starts writing *Tess of the D'Urbervilles* (substantially different from finished novel).

1889 Starts rewriting *Tess of the D'Urbervilles*.

1890 A deterioration in the marriage from here on. 17 March – Tryphena Sparks (Mrs Gale) dies.

1891 Emma starts writing private diary 'What I Think of My Husband' (destroyed by H. after her death). May – A GROUP OF NOBLE DAMES (short stories) published; H. writing most of stories later collected as LIFE'S LITTLE

IRONIES (1894). Nov. – TESS OF THE D'URBERVILLES published, making Hardy a bestseller.

1892 20 July – H.'s father dies. Oct./Dec. – serialization of *The Well-Beloved* (as *The Pursuit of the Well-Beloved*).

1893 19 May – first meets Mrs Florence Henniker, in Dublin.

1894 Dec./Nov. 1895 – serialization of *Jude the Obscure* (as *Hearts Insurgent*).

1895 Nov. – JUDE THE OBSCURE published, with large sales but bitter critical and moral reaction.

1896 Sept. – holiday in Flanders; H. again visits the field of Waterloo. 17 Oct. – a diary note heralds 'the end of prose'.

1897 4 Feb. – diary note planning volume to be called 'Wessex Poems', with sketches by the poet. March – THE WELL-BELOVED published. June – visit to Switzerland.

1898 Dec. – WESSEX POEMS published (collecting poems from 1860s to 1890s).

1899 18 June – meets A. E. Housman. Oct. – outbreak of the South African War, the stimulus for several poems.

1901 Nov. – POEMS OF THE PAST AND THE PRESENT (dated 1902) published and well received. The drafting of *The Dynasts* already begun (begins writing it 1902).

1904 Jan. – THE DYNASTS Part First published. 3 April – H.'s mother dies.

1906 Feb. – THE DYNASTS Part Second published.

1907 Summer – meets Florence Emily Dugdale (second wife).

1908 Feb. – THE DYNASTS Part Third published. This year also sees publication of H.'s edited selection of the poems of William Barnes, and his refusal of a knighthood.

1909 Dec. – TIME'S LAUGHINGSTOCKS (third volume of poetry) published.

1910 Emma finishes writing 'Some Recollections' (private autobiographical memories, later used by H.). July – H. receives the Order of Merit. Nov. – awarded the freedom of Dorchester. Florence Dugdale often at Max Gate.

1912   2 June – (his birthday) Hardy presented with the Gold Medal of the Royal Society of Literature by Henry Newbolt and W. B. Yeats. 27 Nov. – Emma suddenly dies. Dec. – H. starts writing the poems about his relationship with Emma (more than 50 over next two years).

1913   March – visits Plymouth (Emma's birthplace) and north Cornwall: poems inspired by the journey and by Emma's 'Some Recollections'. June – honorary Litt.D., University of Cambridge. Oct. – A CHANGED MAN AND OTHER TALES (stories) published. Nov. – made honorary fellow of Magdalene College, Cambridge.

1914   10 Feb. – marries Florence Dugdale. 4 Aug. – outbreak of First World War. Nov. – SATIRES OF CIRCUMSTANCE (including famous 'Poems of 1912–13' on Emma) published. Nov. – stage adaptation of The Dynasts by Harley Granville-Barker performed.

1915   24 Nov. – Mary Hardy (favourite sister) dies at Talbothays.

1917   H. and Florence start on a 'biography' of the poet. Nov. – MOMENTS OF VISION (fifth vol. of poems) published, and enthusiastically acclaimed.

1920   Honorary D.Litt., University of Oxford. April – last visit to London.

1922   May – LATE LYRICS AND EARLIER published.

1923   Nov. – THE FAMOUS TRAGEDY OF THE QUEEN OF CORNWALL (verse play) published.

1925   Nov. – HUMAN SHOWS (seventh vol. of poems) published.

1927   21 July – last public appearance, laying foundation stone of new buildings of Dorchester Grammar School.

1928   11 Jan. – H. dies; ashes buried in Westminster Abbey, his heart in Emma's grave at Stinsford. Oct. – WINTER WORDS (poems) published. Nov. – THE EARLY LIFE OF THOMAS HARDY published under Florence Hardy's name.

1930   THE LATER YEARS OF THOMAS HARDY and THE COLLECTED POEMS published.

For my parents
'Blessings emblazoned that day'

Introduction

Given that their recurrent themes are those of restrictions, limits, thwartings, there is an irony in the sheer number of poems that Thomas Hardy wrote. Anyone attempting the task of selection is faced with over nine hundred from which to choose. The number could have been even larger: Hardy felt he had destroyed too many of his early poems after failures to publish them in 1866. He published all but a handful of those he subsequently wrote, and in the Preface to the 'Wessex' edition of his works in 1912 he said that if time had allowed he would have wished to write enough in ballad and narrative form to include 'most of the cardinal situations which occur in social and public life' and to encompass, in lyric poetry, 'a round of emotional experiences of some completeness'. At the end of his final volume stands the poem 'He Resolves to Say No More':

> And if my vision range beyond
> The blinkered sight of souls in bond,
>   – By truth made free –
>   I'll let all be,
> And show to no man what I see.

The farewell poets make, and the leave they take, stand against all that they did or didn't leave unsaid. How different the context in which the young William Empson resolved to 'Let it go':

> The contradictions cover such a range.
>   The talk would talk and go so far aslant.
>   You don't want madhouse and the whole thing there.

Not for Hardy any feeling that language couldn't endlessly contain and comment on the world, none of Empson's belief that 'The more things happen to you the more you can't/Tell or remember even what they were'. All poems have their own sense of an ending. Those poems accidentally destined or actually calculated to *stand* at the end have an extra sense: Edward Thomas's 'Out in the Dark', for example, or Tennyson's 'Crossing the Bar' ('Mind you put my "Crossing the Bar" at the end of all editions of my poems'). Empson's appropriate brevity, the quietus of acceptance in the Tennyson and Thomas poems – these contrast with the pressure of the things that could still be 'said' in Hardy's poem. And in Hardy's very title – 'He Resolves to Say No More' – there is the weight also of all that *had* been said.

The 'Victorian' scale of that urge to record and comment on experience looms all the larger when we remember that here also is the author of fifteen novels, an epic drama of Napoleonic Europe (*The Dynasts*), and over forty short stories. The self-consciously relentless awareness of having had forthright things to say brings up at once the question of 'philosophy'. Hardy himself often denied any tidy or logical completeness in his speculations. They were 'really a series of fugitive impressions which I have never tried to co-ordinate'. And this avowal is not to be ignored. It is an earnest of the necessary freedom of the artist within the systems of the thinker. Hardy used the metaphor of the pattern in a carpet: 'by following one colour a certain pattern is suggested, by following another colour, another; so in life the seer should watch that pattern among general things which his idiosyncracy moves him to observe, and describe that alone. This is, quite accurately, a going to Nature; yet the result is no mere photograph, but purely the product of the writer's own mind'. But in reflecting the conditions governing individual, social, and cosmic life, Hardy had not simply challenged the emphases of Victorian Christianity and morality. He had devised philosophical and theological theories, presenting various views of the Power governing the world.

The poem 'Nature's Questioning' conveniently queries the possibilities. Is that Power a 'Vast Imbecility' that has left what it mightily but whimsically created to fend for itself? Is it an 'Automaton', unconscious even of that very act of desertion? Is it possible that the created world itself is the remaining part of a once-conscious Godhead now 'dying downwards' into blindness and unconsciousness? Or is it that there *is* a plan, involving the victory of good over evil, but 'striding over' an uncomprehending world? Apart perhaps from the last, the possibilities strike us as quaint. Even Hardy himself thought the idea of an evil, absconding power 'irresistibly comic', which at least sets him apart from A. E. Housman's 'whatever brute and blackguard made the world'. Such speculations were nevertheless bred out of a sensitivity to human disappointments that is anything but quaint in its range of serious sympathies. Even if the theories qualify only as pseudo-statements, the strength of Hardy's position within them is not to be patronized. They show a refusal to ignore the presence of pain and evil; to ignore (he said, quoting Heine) that the soul has her eternal rights and will 'not be darkened by statutes, nor lullabied by the music of bells'; to ignore 'that if a way to the Better there be, it exacts a full look at the Worst' ('In Tenebris II'). The two dominating ideas are those of an unconscious Immanent Will (writ large in *The Dynasts*) and of a pattern that men just cannot see. In the latter case, human progress – what Hardy calls 'evolutionary meliorism' – would be achieved only through 'loving-kindness' (Christian charity without Christianity's dogma) and the acceptance of a scientific Darwinian rationality that resisted however any reduction of social life to a cold self-seeking. He saw the human race as 'one great network or tissue which quivers in every part when one point is shaken, like a spider's web if touched' and his view embraced all sentient creatures, not just man. Social progress depended on that awareness of organic oneness leading to an acceptance of altruistic responsibilities. A larger, cosmic progress (posited in *The Dynasts*) would depend on this moral sense growing to the point where it informed the unconscious Immanent Will itself. Well, we might say, useful to get that learnt! Hardy's unpatronizable force, however, comes from an imaginative living-into the human needs and sufferings which forced such speculations upon him in the absence of Christian faith. In novels like *The Return of the Native* (1878), *Tess of the D'Urbervilles* (1891) and *Jude the Obscure* (1895) the 'cosmic' shape of things is refracted through social and individual cruelties in ways which increasingly probed and confronted Victorian society. His advanced view of sexual relations in *Jude* brought that theme to the point where it required a D. H. Lawrence – still against public resistance, and with a quarrelsome debt to Hardy – to push it further.

But, born in 1840, the novelist had also been writing poetry since the mid-1860s. Eventually Hardy came to argue that it was as a poet he had always seen himself. He first planned an actual volume of verse in 1892, and turned completely from novel writing after the publication of *Jude* in 1895. The hostile moral reaction to that novel (despite its large sales) certainly weighed in the decision. But it cannot be divorced from the fact that the sheer effort of novel writing had already become more difficult, complicated as it was by ill-health and depression in the 1880s and by the deterioration of his relationship with his first wife from around 1890. A diary note of October 1896 recording 'the end of prose' was soon followed by another planning a collection of poems from the period since 1865. Running his controversial themes poetically underground wasn't the motive, though Hardy did write that 'If Galileo had said in verse [as opposed to 'argumentative prose'] that the world moved, the Inquisition might have let him alone'. And he said of his own poetry that, 'unlike some of the fiction, nothing interfered with the writer's freedom in respect of its form or content'. A morally independent stance just isn't as dangerously fleshed out in verse. But in Hardy's verse it didn't need to be flushed out, either. The same attitudes, along with their philosophical or theological bases, remain clear and uncompromising. Those poems which cross-examine God and his motives ('Milton made God argue' – Hardy once quoted Bagehot's comment as epigraph) don't have Milton's epic and biblical scale as cover.

But this isn't, on its own, what makes the poetry's appeal survive. For survive it has done, on a slow fuse, into our own time. *Wessex Poems* (1898) was the first of eight volumes – the last published posthumously in 1928, the year of Hardy's death – that were to span a period of major changes in English poetry. Unlike W. B. Yeats, however, Hardy did not forge a new major voice out of the new historical and literary flux of that period. There is no equivalent question in his case to the one we ask regarding Yeats, 'How many miles from Innisfree to Byzantium?' Indeed, the seamlessness of Hardy's poetic output when we consider the quality and kind of his best poems, early and late, is part of the phenomenon he represents. It is a consistency of style as much as of vision and preoccupation, enabling us to see him as the poet who most successfully relayed the native English tradition of the nineteenth century into the twentieth. During the thirty years of the poetry's publication, it was a younger and different breed of poets who had to battle against what Hardy called 'inert crystallized opinion'. And that battle itself had more to do with style than with immediately controversial content. Hardy's kind of poetry stands over against the Modernist poetic revolution effected between 1910 and 1930 by poets like Eliot and Pound. That revolution had its roots in a continental 'Symbolist' tradition of the late nineteenth century which also brought a different poet like Yeats into the picture. Whereas their kind of poetry – allusive, mythopoeic, more obviously irreducible – once appeared to have superannuated Hardy's significance, a longer time-scale has since then readjusted our view. In his book *Thomas Hardy and British Poetry* (1973) Donald Davie explores, and confirms, the thesis 'that in British poetry of the last fifty years (as not in American) the most far-reaching influence, for good and ill, has been not Yeats, still less Eliot or Pound, not Lawrence, but *Hardy*'.

This is a remarkable testimony. For one thing Hardy's influence, and that of any poetry that had its roots deep in the English nineteenth century, was interrupted by the death of a young generation of poets in the Great War. That war also forced a major shift in sensibility, a psychological transformation later recorded with frightening understatement in Philip Larkin's poem 'MCMXIV' – 'Never such innocence again'. The poetic modernism of T. S. Eliot wasn't formed out of that fact ('Prufrock', for example, dates from 1910). But the kind of verse that Eliot wrote – culturally, emotionally, and narratively dislocated – was to seem better suited to capture the condition of post-World War experience. The impression of Hardy as simply a survivor, as opposed to those who like Eliot and Pound consciously strove to 'alter expression' and 'make it new', would have been confirmed by a comparison of Hardy's volumes of 1917 and 1922 with Eliot's *Prufrock and Other Observations* and *The Waste Land* of the same respective years. And Hardy's view that free verse 'would come to nothing in England' highlights his own relentlessly traditional sense of form as it lay at the heart of the contrast. 'All we can do', he said, 'is to write on the old themes in the old styles, but try to do a little better than those who went before us.'

Yet there is no finer example of the relay of poetic impulse from one generation to another than that which had already crossed from Hardy's 'In the Time of "The Breaking of Nations" ' to Edward Thomas's 'As the Team's Headbrass'. Thomas's measuring of the madness of war against the creative processes of the English countryside maintains Hardy's exact associations without tying Thomas to Hardy's verseform, diction, or sensibility. Thomas's increasing reputation in our own time is part of the picture that has emerged since the 1930s, more clearly than would have been possible in the 1920s, of an available alternative to the more obviously striking experimentation of the Modernists. But even those poets of the Great War less naturally in the line of Hardy (Wilfred Owen or Isaac Rosenberg, for example) had shown that it was possible to register a new sensibility not through consciously revolutionary techniques but in simpler revolt against the outrage done to ordinary human life and values.

In this sense it is not Hardy's war poems that evoke the essential affinity. After all, 'In the Time of "The Breaking of Nations" ', though written during the Great War, took its source from the Franco-Prussian War of 1870; and its rural reflexes would have been individually, temperamentally, attractive to Edward Thomas. It must also be stressed that those poems Hardy actually wrote on the Great War included 'recruitment' pieces of pride and valour. That was the kind of response that the increasing cruelties of the war made untenable. Even in 1914 one such Hardy poem, 'Men Who March Away', though praised by Edward Thomas, had been attacked for its traditional patriotism by Charles Sorley, a poet who otherwise admired Hardy. But the point is that the outraged response to war of Sorley, Owen, or Siegfried Sassoon was already in the broader humane tradition of other Hardy poems, with their pained attacks on a world ruled, apparently, by an unthinking or unfeeling Power. Sassoon actually said that his satirical war poems could claim only Hardy as a model, and the Hardy poems he specified were *Satires of Circumstance*, published in 1914, although the Boer War had produced a more obviously Sassoon-like poem in 'The Man He Killed'. It is the democratic force of that wider vision – bad theology but understandable feelings – that survived through Hardy. And survived *in* him: 'After two thousand years of mass/We've got as far as poison-gas': the date of those lines (1924) now makes us see them as if also linking *back* to Sassoon; just as a comparison of Hardy's 'Unkept Good Fridays' forwards to Kingsley Amis's 'New Approach Needed' shows the legacy of that readiness to cross from outrage into sacrilege reaching our own time.

It was in a very different way that the poetry of Yeats, Eliot or Pound confronted historic and personal events, merging them in a wider perspective that mixed different orders of experience, different periods, and different cultures. Hardy's more traditionally democratic procedure, responding discretely to ordinary events and experiences in a sequential world of time, is also as if reinforced by the unusually wide variety of verse-forms he employed. Unlike Yeats or Eliot, he offers no sense of the possibility of achieving revelation through the vertical penetration of one masterful voice, the perfection of major symbols, or the general triumph of style over experience. More appropriate would be Robert Frost's view of a poem as being only 'a momentary stay against confusion'. This provisional quality is as if further reflected by the fact that many of Hardy's verse-forms do not appear totally inevitable, by his apparent infelicities of phrasing, and his choice of certain grotesque words. Hardy attacked his earliest reviewers for ascribing these 'to ignorance' when they were 'really choice after full knowledge'. And the same goes for what seems at first the awkward movement of so much of the verse. The character-ful music of 'To Lizbie Browne', for example, shows a won-derful counterpointing of the spoken voice against any lazy rhythmic expectations. Hardy's view was that 'the whole secret of a living style and the difference between it and a dead style, lies in not having too much style'. As with the novels (bad architecture, marvellous gargoyles), an unem-barrassed ruggedness remains.

These aspects of the poetry's perspective and perfor-mance remained at the heart of Hardy's appeal for the young poets who emerged in the 1930s. He was Dylan Thomas's 'favourite' poet: the word is significant. Equally revealing is W. H. Auden's claim that it was through reading Hardy that he first thought it possible to write poetry himself, and the work of a lesser poet like C. Day Lewis (or the older Edmund Blunden) was to reveal Hardy as a constantly influential model. No doubt, even in the 1930s, this was because of the more obviously daunting example of the Modernists, whose experimentations must at the same time have seemed to be the result of their 'outsider' relationship to English society. The impersonality and scale of the American Eliot's literary-cultural allusiveness, for example, or of the Irish Yeats's occult system of symbols, contrast with Hardy's quiet atten-tion to distinct ordinary experiences. His unreal talk about the 'First Cause' or 'Immanent Will' derives its acceptability from what is already a rich immersion in real joys and fears. Central to his poems is the human scale that they maintain. 'He was a man who used to notice such things': that instinct had been bred early and deep in this product of rural Dorsetshire. The upward social mobility that came with the novelist's fame or with the autodidact's increasing 'knowledge' did not change that perspective.

In a still later generation, Hardy's importance was forthrightly asserted by Philip Larkin, clearly one of the finest of the poets who came into prominence in the 1950s. It was indicated not only by the Hardyan influence at work in Larkin's own poetry (in 'Love Songs in Age' for example) but by Larkin's unequivocal judgment that Hardy's *Collected Poems* represented 'many times over the best body of poetic work this century so far has to show'. This enthusiasm no doubt reflects something even further levelled-down in the nature and temperament of English society since 1945. Certainly, from this distance, the intellectual-hierarchical 'authority' of Yeats or Eliot or Pound (seen increasingly as posing 'political' as well as stylistic problems) can appear alien. By the 1950s even the different, 'bardic' archness of a Dylan Thomas was seen by the younger poets of the *New Lines* anthologies as something to be undercut. Of course, this view of Hardy's survival, as seen against the more obviously dramatic revolution of the Modernists, could be rehearsed in such a way as to bring out contradictions and different confirmations. Thus we remember Pound's own admiration for Hardy – 'Now *there* is a clarity. There *is* the harvest of having written 20 novels first.' In any case, in speaking of 'alternative' traditions in modern poetry, we run the danger of recognizing only the influence of Hardy as standing over against that of the Modernists. A quite different alternative line, for example, exploring more elementally the world of birds, beasts and flowers, would run from D. H. Lawrence to Ted Hughes. Nevertheless, the phenomenon remains: the influence of a poet born in 1840, whose poetry did not need to change in the last thirty years of his life to become quietly potent in the subsequent fifty years of this century. Its sheer bulk makes a selection useful, setting the massiveness in relief. What is to be avoided is any distortion of perspective. F. R. Leavis, though powerfully praising a poem like 'After a Journey', insisted that Hardy's greatness rested on only a dozen such poems. Philip Larkin, whose first volume bore uncomfortably the mark of Yeats, dated a new inspiration from when he first read Hardy's 'Thoughts of Phena at News of Her Death', but also claimed that 'one reader at least would not wish Hardy's *Collected Poems* a single page shorter'. Somewhere between these two views, we need to ask again, 'What kind of poetry did Hardy write?' Its stature and influence seem puzzling in the light of its relative unadventurousness. Donald Davie claimed that 'None of Hardy's admirers have yet found how to make Hardy the poet *weigh* equally with Eliot and Pound and Yeats.'

What does one make of a poem like this, for example? –

Nobody Comes

Tree-leaves labour up and down,
    And through them the fainting light
    Succumbs to the crawl of night.
Outside in the road the telegraph wire
    To the town from the darkening land
Intones to travellers like a spectral lyre
    Swept by a spectral hand.

A car comes up, with lamps full-glare,
    That flash upon a tree:
    It has nothing to do with me,
And whangs along in a world of its own,
    Leaving a blacker air;
And mute by the gate I stand again alone,
    And nobody pulls up there.

It seems so slight, and slightly awkward. Even against its two highly structured stanzas, it leaves an impression of a raw experience hardly worked upon. Yet it is a poem that will not easily let us go. The happy selection of 'whangs' to describe the car brings to the surface an authenticity of response that inheres in more than just that word. The telegraph wire and the car (both, ironically, means of communication) register an impersonal modernity. Yet they appear less exaggerated and more authentic than, say, the aerodromes, pylons, and other industrial antipoetic props of the 1930s. Less exaggerated, but not unstated: 'It has nothing to do with me.' The appropriate image does not displace the poetry of emotive statement. Our sense of a poem's traditional proportions is maintained. We feel that a recognizable emotional condition actually exists, and *gathers round* the appropriate images, in which the poet's emotion finds its depth but not its total expression. 'The most prosaic man becomes a poem when you stand by his grave at his funeral and think of him.' It is against that kind of Wordsworthian belief that 'Nobody Comes', as much as more obviously finished poems, demands attention. Hardy claimed that 'There is a latent music in the sincere utterance of deep emotion, however expressed, which fills the place of the actual word-music in rhythmic phraseology on thinner emotive subjects, or on subjects with next to none at all . . . This suggested conception seems to me to be the only one which explains all cases, including those instances of verse that apparently infringe all rules, and yet bring unreasoned convictions that they are poetry.'

'Nobody Comes': the poet who wrote that poem was eighty-four years old. Old age's law of diminishing returns might adequately explain its blankness. But variations of the phrase 'nobody comes' echo throughout Hardy's poems, most resonantly in 'A Broken Appointment' – 'You did not come,/And marching Time drew on, and wore me numb'. Literal broken appointments, those non-events, real and imagined, are experiences the novelist in Hardy is very good on. One of the most poignant things about the 1912–13 poems on the death of his first wife, Emma, is the way the idea of the broken appointment, now beyond any simple blame, survives as metaphor. It is nicely pointed in 'The Voice':

> Can it be you that I hear? Let me view you, then,
> Standing as when I drew near to the town
> Where you would wait for me: yes, as I knew you then,
> Even to the original air-blue gown!

But a more general feel of blankness, of being as it were outside experience as well as outside experiences, is there in Hardy from the beginning. It involves of course the question of Belief or beliefs, of appointments that were in his case never made. The feel of not to feel it: 'The Impercipient', 'In Tenebris', 'The Oxen' or 'The Darkling Thrush' show how this general blankness *attends on*, as well as grows out of, the poetry's occasions. The images for it are perhaps most memorable when it is indeed more individual losses, especially that of Emma, that distil them. In a great poem like 'The Going' for example: 'while I/Saw morning harden upon the wall,/Unmoved, unknowing . . .' and 'I seem but a dead man held on end/To sink down soon . . .' 'Blankness' is in fact a word in 'The Going'. It reminds us, however, of an earlier and different poem where it occurs:

> The railway bore him through
> An earthen cutting out from a city:
> There was no scope for view,
> Though the frail light shed by a slim young moon
> Fell like a friendly tune.
>
> Fell like a liquid ditty,
> And the blank lack of any charm
> Of landscape did no harm.
> The bald steep cutting, rigid, rough,
> And moon-lit, was enough
> For poetry of place: its weathered face
> Formed a convenient sheet whereon
> The visions of his mind were drawn.

An uncannily modern poem, once again its modernity does not rest in any obvious antipoetic advantage taken of its impersonal 'railway' setting. The featureless scene is certainly described, but it is also more indirectly worked into our consciousness. This is because the optimistic imagination which momentarily transcends that scene is itself cut across: by the self-critical force of the words 'convenient' and 'visions', for example, and the way in which the whole poem is circumscribed by its very title – 'After a *Romantic* Day'. And yet the 'romantic' transcendence of actuality is not vandalized. The poem's layered circumspection seems a finer thing than the flattened-out choices in, say, Matthew Arnold's 'Dover Beach':

> for the world, which seems
> To lie before us like a land of dreams,
> So various, so beautiful, so new,
> Hath really neither joy, nor love, nor light . . .

Even in its under-reaching, Hardy's poem sensitively communicates what is also Arnold's belief: that the world derives its meaning only from the energies, loyalties or memories that we bring to it. The animist world of the Romantics being dead, the Victorian loss also of a Christian certainty underlies the potential blankness. But that loss did not keep Hardy in the grip of a 'public' rhetoric. This was largely because his lyric poems quickly developed an anecdotal concreteness, whether their occasions were personal or what he often called 'impersonative' or fictional. Hardy could have echoed Arnold's boast about his poetry expressing 'the main movement of mind' of his generation. But the 'public spokesman' quality of Arnold's 'Marguerite' poems or his 'Resignation: To Fausta' is in Hardy domesticated, in a strong sense of anecdotal immediacy. The influence of George Meredith's *Modern Love* sonnets, combining the language of contemporary ideas with that of a love relationship, was similarly strengthened in Hardy's own early sonnets by the communication of the claustrophobic feel of such a relationship. Hardy's 'Revulsion' or the 'She to Him' sequence, for example, remain strangely powerful sonnets – 'Numb as a vane that cankers on its point' – despite their Shakespearean stylization.

Naturally, in substance as well as style, the ballad and narrative poems will seem at first more remote than the kind of poem so far mentioned. But that it is in their case a *social* remoteness reminds us of something important about Hardy. Such ballad and folk materials were not artificially reached for. They represented for Hardy the very feel of the actual rural community in which he grew up. Not only its habits, personalities, and textures but its own ability to celebrate these in tales, superstitions, and songs. In that sense, generations lay articulately as well as tangibly behind generations. It is significant, for example, that he considered 'A Trampwoman's Tragedy' to be one of his finest poems, and lyrics about members of his own immediate family singing or telling stories bring this 'ballad' dimension really home. His poem on refusing 'An Invitation to the United States' pleads his need to stay in touch with a community 'scored with prints of perished hands' and to 'Give past exemplars present room,/And their experience count as mine'. Those very lines, however, hint at a duality. The kind of material exercised in the ballad-type poems shows a society rich in its connections with the imagination of the past through folk traditions and even actual historic memory ('he can call up the French Revolution!'), and rich also in the physical remains of much earlier and different civilizations. The duality comes in the accompanying feeling that the society itself was passing. Rural Dorset seemed a place proper to grow wise in, if only that so many dead lay round.

It is of course possible to sentimentalize the passing of that world. Hardy, revealing his own need, was exaggerating when he claimed that sophisticated London ballads had slain the authentic rural ones 'at a stroke'. In any case, he himself in some ways grew socially and intellectually away from the community from which those ballads sprang. He constructed a family tree that tended to obscure the more purely peasant aspects of his origins, and his poems show quite early on that they can reflect the world of provincial gentility – of fashionable seaside towns and cathedral cities – as comfortably as they do the peasant hinterland. He was eventually to grow, in social terms, even further away from his first world. As a member of fashionable London society, of the Savile and Atheneum clubs, and a regular attender with Emma at the annual social 'seasons', the later Hardy could even call himself 'half a Londoner'. This is the Hardy so delightfully portrayed in the after-dinner-speech idiom of the poem 'An Ancient to Ancients' – with the obvious, and honourable, relish of the self-made man. The very architecture and respectability of Max Gate, the house he designed for himself in 1883, although only a few miles from the cottage of his childhood, reflected that sense of having arrived.

Nevertheless, the slow passing of his first peasant world (the finally 'darkening land' of 'Nobody Comes'?) was all along felt as a loss of connection. That very perception of course depended on Hardy's social ability to stand, to some degree, apart. In the poems, the threat of loss is not necessarily a matter of specific statement; Hardy is more obviously the sad historian of the pensive plain in his novels. What is significant in the poems is how much they still share in the social world of the novels, with something like the same kind of memorializing attentiveness, and at a time when the more central fashions of Victorian poetry had set quite different norms. In the case of the ballad and narrative poems as such, it is as if Hardy needed to take life not only from the imagining of his society but from the very imagination of that society itself: those were the kinds of tales they told. But the same imaginative need seems also true, in a different way, of countless shorter poems which might otherwise strike us as not having any particularly urgent point or narrative interest at all. In these poems, we come to feel that it is the atmosphere of a particular place and people that holds the poet, more than any anecdotal quiddity or satire of circumstance as such. The lone woman at a miserably rained-out fair in 'Expectation and Experience', for example, fascinates him as much as the more fully patterned events of the longer narratives. In comparison, those poems in Words-worth's *Lyrical Ballads* which stand in the same tradition have much more obvious and complicated moral designs upon us. Hardy seems movingly content with a poetry of ordinariness, and in the upshot seems closer than Words-worth to the actual sensibility of those who people the poet's world.

This kind of material, and Hardy's response to it, affected the style and method even of the lyrics proper. If Hardy does not seem to us in those lyrics an abstracting sage on the mid-Victorian model, and if he did not succumb to the stylis-tic dreaminess of the poetry of the 1890s (which he saw as prettily expressing unimportant things), it is because some-thing in him resisted the thinning of ordinary realistic tex-ture, and more importantly of a sense of *situation*, that could have accompanied the loss of larger certainties. The man who lost his Christian faith, to some degree under the influence of Darwinism, remained a 'churchy' poet – with a deeply absorbed knowledge of the Bible, of hymns and psalm tunes, and of church customs and architecture that amounts to something more solid than awkward reverence. Above all, a feeling for individual contingent lives was fed from a particular rural community through the novels and narrative poems into the lyric poetry itself. The essentially regional character of that source of power is something that poets of the last fifty years have had to rediscover after the cosmopolitanism of Modernism. Even Gerard Manley Hopkins, Hardy's exact contemporary but culturally his diametric opposite, found regional dialects and landscapes a necessary resource against Victorian poetic styles. Hardy was not completely halted within his first world as was his exact co-regionalist, his beloved William Barnes, but the grittiness of some of his diction and syntax remained, as much as actual dialect words, the sign of something that ran very deep indeed in his fellow-feeling with Barnes. It is from this kind of base that we can also understand why Browning (a poet whose Christian optimism Hardy thought pathetic) could influence him, whereas Swinburne (whom he in some ways admired more) left no mark. Neither of those poets represented anything like the world from which Hardy sprang. But Browning's quirkiness in diction, syntax, and way of telling a story had a texture that sorted naturally with Hardy's materials, whereas the purer music of Swinburne or Tennyson (or Shelley – the lyric poet Hardy most admired) did not.

A sense of cultural belonging, threatened by the vanishing of a society and a changing self, was something Hardy had increasingly to find through memory. And it may be that, in turn, the role of memory itself links the ballads and ballad-type poems to the lyrics, including the greater ones, as if there were a cultural or otherwise wider dimension to those more personally felt poems. It is certainly remarkable that so many of the lyrics should be in the first place about memory and memories, about events at the point of loss, as if in fear of a colourless present. Retrospection became the natural habit of his soul. It is as if, whatever the theme or type of poem, he 'cannot but remember such things were,/ That were most precious to him'. Few poets are as naturally elegiac as Hardy; or since that word brings up the case of Tennyson, few in whom the elegiac tendency is not just a diffused mood but a necessary way of seeing – refocusing and clinging to individual things in *personal* as well as social life ('even to the original air-blue gown'!). Quite apart from its larger scale, a poem like Wordsworth's *Prelude* trawls the personal past more obviously out of psychological and cultural need. But the same kind of need also seems true of Hardy, and this naturally retrospective tendency appears all the more significant when we realize that we think at once, in Hardy's case, not of childhood but of adult experiences retrieved.

It is, however, to a poem of childhood memory that we shall turn to suggest that there is indeed a cultural dimension to this natural recourse to memory. That poem is 'The Self-Unseeing'. Behind its force as an example lie many other poems in which personal memories and those of others merge, and merge the generations. Their mutuality – their sense of the shared details of place, character, and talent – links the poet to a wider web of feeling. (Examples would be 'Domicilium', 'A Church Romance', 'Friends Beyond', 'Voices from Things Growing in a Churchyard', 'To My Father's Violin', 'Old Furniture', 'One We Knew'.) Here is 'The Self-Unseeing':

> Here is the ancient floor,
> Footworn and hollowed and thin,
> Here was the former door
> Where the dead feet walked in.
>
> She sat here in her chair,
> Smiling into the fire;
> He who played stood there,
> Bowing it higher and higher.
>
> Childlike I danced in a dream;
> Blessings emblazoned that day;
> Everything glowed with a gleam;
> Yet we were looking away!

This seems to me one of the finest short poems in the language. It richly evokes the importance Hardy attached to what he called 'the wear on a threshold', the essentially *human* importance of places, the equivalent of Keats's 'nature is fine, but human nature is finer'. An interesting comparison would be with D. H. Lawrence's poem 'Piano'. The strength of Hardy's poem however is that it is naturally free of the simple regressiveness of nostalgia, which Lawrence had to disinfect more pointedly by saying that 'the glamour of *child-ish* days is upon me'. The strange inaccuracy of Hardy's word 'childlike' – after all, he *was* a child – is in fact a strength, supporting rather than supplanting the glow and gleam. For it is a more complex human limitation than mere nostalgia that the poem identifies, one that is as characteristic of the adult as of the child ('*we* were looking away'). It is the paradox that experience is in one sense most ungraspable while still within our grasp. This understanding of the natural gap between possession and self-possession is central to the nature of Hardy's poetry. It is there in 'In Front of the Landscape' whose more conventional concern with ghosts does not obscure its understanding of the same phenomenon: that 'the intenser stare of the mind' is only possible in retrospect. For a moment, in 'The Self-Unseeing', a layer of guilt has been lifted off the perception, by the luminous thankfulness of the elegy. And by a poised matter-of-factness, too: the 'former door' of Hardy's birthplace was indeed a door bricked up since Hardy's childhood; and he and his parents in the poem are also quite literally 'looking away' – into the fire, or upwards with the violin, or in the whirl of the boy's dance. That matter-of-factness is crucial to the poem's deepest significance. That is to say, it is the domestic actuality of the boy's dance that moves us. The idea of the dance became Yeats's great symbol for possession by experience ('How can we know the dancer from the dance?'), while in Eliot it became a more intellectualized necessity, 'where you must move in measure like a dancer'. That thinning-out of the social reality of the dance emphasizes the way in which, in 'The Self-Unseeing', it is simply the natural activity of a culture, a once unselfconscious way of life. And the point is that, in such a poem, cultural and personal memories achieve identity. Despite Lawrence's 'childish days' there also comes in 'Piano' a similar sense of cultural belonging – of which the trans-Atlantic Eliot's insult (later regretted) about 'hymn-singing pietism' could be only a brutal caricature. One remembers Henry James's jibe about 'the good little Thomas Hardy'.

'Today has length, breadth, thickness, colour, smell, voice. As soon as it becomes *yesterday* it is a thin layer among many layers, without substance, colour, or articulate sound.' Hardy's abstract diary comment of January 1897 rehearses the personal texture and 'substance' that are lost when the possessing present becomes the past. Repossession in more than a fleeting sense is one of the creative possibilities of language; but for a man who felt intellectually 'born out of due time' the enterprise became a necessity as well as a fine art. The past was needed to reinforce a sense of reality and value in the present. Also to be traced in the poems of memory, however, is the wisdom which that self-possessed recollection brings. The range of urgencies represented by this impulse to cut back into experience in its earlier or vanishing forms is wide, and measures the range of Hardy's imagination. Ironically, that range itself now confounds time: too many of Hardy's poems are undatable to provide any tidy chronology. But if we trace, spirally as it were, the different ways in which Hardy probes time, the pattern leads us towards his finest poems, and upwards within them.

At the lowest level, there is the kind of poem in which the potentialities of memory are quite simply celebrated. 'One We Knew', for example, on his grandmother's memorializing talents:

> She would dwell on such themes, not as one who
> remembers
> But rather as one who sees . . .
>
> Past things retold were to her as things existent,
> Things present but as a tale.

The delight here, both within and outside the poem's frame, is the basic one of the teller and the tale, that of the ballads and the narrative poems – though the latter of course, like the novels and short stories, give the poet and reader a god-like view of what the past and future keep from the present. A different tremor naturally enters when the memories gather round an actual life that has more crucially touched Hardy's own. And even amongst those poems there are varying degrees to which the poet makes real that difference between simply 'remembering' and (in its many senses) 'seeing'. But the power of even the best, the 1912–13 elegies for example, is still related to the basic one of all good literature, fictive as well as confessional: the ability to gain, in George Eliot's phrase, 'a superadded life in the life of others'.

That George Eliot was referring to human relationships rather than the novel form as such is to the point. It relates the moral needs of life to the moral opportunities of art. A crucial feature of Hardy's poems about Emma (and they include many more than just those dated '1912–13') is their urge to 'see' even more than can be literally remembered. It is this completeness of effort that impresses. The poem 'Places', for example, gives to scenes from Emma's life even before Hardy knew her 'a savour that scenes in being lack,/ And a presence more than the actual brings'. Here again, as in 'One We Knew' above, it is the present that seems a 'tale'. But the border crossed is not only that between 'then' and 'now'. It is more fully that between 'me' and *'you'*. It is *this* possibility that arose from the visit to Cornwall after Emma's death and the availability of her own independent diary 'Recollections', that explains the need for so many poems, and the power of even the lesser ones. Hardy's imagination reaches not only into Emma's single days but into her own vantage-point, both before the first meeting ('A Man Was Drawing Near to Me') and after death itself ('The Haunter'). Alun Lewis, imagining his wife after his own death in 'Song: On Seeing Dead Bodies Floating Off the Cape', traversed psychology and time as if they had the same border, experiencing 'the nearness that is waiting in my bed' as powerfully as 'the gradual self-effacement of the dead'. 'My Spirit Will Not Haunt the Mound', spoken by Emma, per-suades us that a similar 'me/you' division has been under-stood, and crossed. The dead Emma is allowed to turn on Hardy the most delicate of challenges:

> And there you'll find me, if a jot
> >   You still should care
> For me, and for my curious air;
> If otherwise, then I shall not,
> >   For you, be there.

Those two words *for you* are beautifully levered by rhythm and punctuation, and their accusation is deepened by the applicability of the last two lines to the cold relationship of the last twenty years at Max Gate. The death was of one who had already been allowed to go.

The awareness of things ill done, and done to others' harm: the coldness from Hardy's side had its source in a curious kind of self-absorption. He seems to have been in the first place a man whose sensitivity was expressed more easily in his work than in his daily dealings with others. Even in his writings he shows an interest in certain ideas that might be called the ideas of selfishness. In poems like 'At a Bridal' and 'To a Motherless Child', as also in *Jude the Obscure*, his attack on personal fate and society involves thoughts about eugenics and asexual birth. The survival of the best or the personally meaningful, as exclusively decided upon by Hardy, was something that Nature and the nature of things did not allow. 'To a Motherless Child', for example, laments that the survival in her child of Hardy's greatest love before Emma, his cousin Tryphena Sparks, had been 'alloyed': the daughter did not exactly reproduce Tryphena. One diary entry even delights in viewing a literary work as being Hardy's 'child' alone. Some such obsession also remained behind the most suitable irony of all: that Hardy, a poet so concerned with ghosts, should have ghost-written his second wife's 'biography' of him. A real biography would have meant that his own interpretation of himself was negotiable, could be differently fleshed, would be 'alloyed'.

But this negative impulse intensified positive talents. Philip Larkin's Hardy-like lines can remind us of them:

> Truly, though our element is time,
> We are not suited to the long perspectives
> Open at each instant of our lives.
> They link us to our losses: worse,
> They show us what we have as it once was,
> Blindingly undiminished, just as though
> By acting differently we could have kept it so.

The point is that Hardy, as poet, *is* suited to those long perspectives that link him to his losses. The greater generosity of the poems on Emma draw on the same genius for intense retrieval as serves those losses that are more selfishly relished. He once spoke of his faculty 'for burying an emotion in my heart or brain for forty years, and exhuming it at the end of that time as fresh as when interred'. 'Blindingly undiminished': Larkin's phrase reminds us that Hardy is good on those visual details that pin memories without pinning them down dead –

> The smile on your face was the deadest thing
> Alive enough to have strength to die
> ('Neutral Tones')

> Her laugh was not in the middle of her face quite
> ('A Countenance')

>   her foot near mine on the bending limb,
> Laughing, her young brown arm awave
> ('Logs on the Hearth').

And that grasp of the visual is also there in his descriptions of nature, most significantly when it has to be reached for through mist or dusk, and when the very rhythms have therefore to be a part of the perception:

> Ancient chalk-pit, milestone, rills in the grass-flat
>   Stroked by the light,
> Seemed but a ghost-like gauze
> ('In Front of the Landscape')

> If it be in the dusk when, like an eyelid's soundless blink,
>   The dewfall-hawk comes crossing the shades to alight
> Upon the wind-warped upland thorn
> ('Afterwards').

For it is not a photographic matching that is sought. That particular art grew up with Hardy, and the monochrome, neutral tones of so many of the poems maybe reflect that fact. He even has a poem about a photograph. But a Larkin poem about photographs tells us what we need to remember also about still memories in the mind: they 'lacerate/Simply by being over'. Worse, 'what was/Won't call on us to justify/Our grief'. The memories need to be more fully re-imagined. Otherwise, memory is not knowledge and will not lead us to deeper truths. Hardy made the comment about a different art: 'I don't want to see landscapes, i.e., scenic paintings of them, because I don't want to see the original realities – as optical effects that is. I want to see the deeper reality underlying the scenic, the expression of what are sometimes called abstract imaginings.' In 'Thoughts of Phena' he refers to those pre-industrial mementos that photography ultimately replaced: 'Not a line of her writing have I,/Not a thread of her hair . . . whereby I may *picture* her there'. But he believes that the 'best of her' is all the more meaningfully retained, 'fined in my brain', because of the *absence* of such literally detachable relics.

It is this greater kind of detachability, this 'deeper reality' gleaned from the past, that conditions or transforms the present. The problem in poetry is how most fully to com-municate its influence. The intensity with which the language preserves and reorganizes the original experiences is of course crucial. A past that is not intensely re-imagined will give no base for the feelings of loss or change that a poem sets out to express. That vivid base guards the poem's medita-tive parts against the effects of being mere assertion. But the meditation and reflection still face the danger of appearing inadequate, less intensely persuasive than the recollections on which they are based.

This was a particular danger for Hardy, whose poetry is in any case, in the main, a poetry of statement, that of 'a man speaking to men', in the syntactic sense of Wordsworth's formula. Indeed, much of what made Hardy once seem unmodern had to do with just that discursive deployment of his verse. As part of his early self-education he had even set himself to analyse the style of the leader-writers of *The Times*. Even in his finest poems, we see signs of where a ponderous, discursive syntax has had to be wilfully contracted to fit the rhythms and line-lengths of predetermined stanza-forms. In 'Thoughts of Phena', for example –

> yet haply the best of her – fined in my brain
> It may be the more
> That no line of her writing have I . . .

Or in the second of these two lines from 'Neutral Tones' –

> And some words played between us to and fro
> On which lost the more by our love.

The discursiveness itself, however, the language of self-possession, cannot be divorced from the poetry's earnest honesty. Hardy, the former architect, drew an analogy with architecture – 'both arts, unlike some others, having to carry a rational content inside their artistic form'. And in any case loose-limbed syntax, suddenly contracted, can provide its own intensities. The stanza from 'My Spirit Will Not Haunt the Mound' above was an example, as are these lines from 'Molly Gone':

> Thinking thus, there's a many-flamed star in the air,
> That tosses a sign
> That her glance is regarding its face from her home, so that there
> Her eyes may have meetings with mine.

Hardy is imagining that his dead sister and he are reunited in the act of observing the same star. Both 'its face' and 'there' refer to the star. But it is difficult to avoid strangely beautiful misreadings: 'her glance is regarding its face' and 'her home, so that *there* . . .' After the open discursiveness of what precedes them ('Where, then, is Molly, who's no more with me?') the lines seem all the more magical. Syntax also has its ghosts.

Some of Hardy's finest poems, however, actually enact a withdrawal from the open syntax of discourse and description. That they are often claimed to be the *very* finest may have something to do with our liking for the imagistic and irreducible in poetry. Poems like 'Snow in the Suburbs' and

'The Darkling Thrush' show images almost crowding out the act of description as such – but Hardy still remains narratively amongst his images in both. Other poems, however, enact a search for images placed, as it were, beyond comment. Being poems of memory, they reflect the stylistic as well as the emotive tensions of that rending pain of re-enactment at the core of Hardy's power. By finding final images for the bereft present, he achieves an intensity beyond the reach of the more openly emotive expression that we associate with discursive syntax. One feels that this is a central human need. Unless we 'see' the final images of our pain as clearly as the things still 'blindingly undiminished' in the past, our self-possession gutters, we are really in the dark.

The earliest of three poems we shall look at (its date – 1867 – still amazes) is 'Neutral Tones'. It is magnificently and openly descriptive, but its greatness is in the way it gathers its own images finally into 'shapes' rather than 'lessons', and does so at the very point where it overreaches the sonnet's traditional length:

> Since then, keen lessons that love deceives,
> And wrings with wrong, have shaped to me
> Your face, and the God-curst sun, and a tree,
> And a pond edged with grayish leaves.

Rhythm, as well as the images 'shaped', have in those last two lines *become* meaning. In 'The Voice' we see the shape of the poem itself contracting. Its first three stanzas match their interrogative leisure with long lines, the dactyllic rhythm and triple-rhymes allowing alternate lines to carry twelve syllables across their four stresses. Then the final stanza:

> Thus I; faltering forward,
> Leaves around me falling,
> Wind oozing thin through the thorn from norward,
> And the woman calling.

Modulation isn't the right word for what has happened there. Contraction is; and the straitening is as if mocked by the one surviving long line, which recoups however only ten syllables and carries the thinnest words. Verbs reduced to participles reinforce the imagistic impact. Hardy 'sees' himself. That sense of loss which in other poems befell a life remembered spatially as *'largest, best'*, and *'altered* all', is here itself physically seen in the act of altering. It is a poetry alive enough to have strength to die.

The altering remains literally a matter of endings in 'During Wind and Rain'. Now it is the repeated alteration in the endings of individual stanzas. But there are other endings before those, *within* the stanzas. In each stanza what we have is a movement through luminously beautiful scenes from Emma's life before she knew Hardy. These peter out, wistfully at first, in dots; then in what threatens to be an inadequate sigh; and finally in a line that finds in its autonomous image the only adequate correlative for the emotion seeking expression in the whole:

> They are blithely breakfasting all –
> Men and maidens – yea,
> Under the summer tree,
> With a glimpse of the bay,
> While pet fowl come to the knee . . .
> Ah, no; the years O!
> And the rotten rose is ript from the wall.

Even the final lines themselves, when viewed together, mime this progress towards an image beyond comment:

> How the sick leaves reel down in throngs!
>
> See, the white storm-birds wing across!
>
> And the rotten rose is ript from the wall.
>
> Down their carved names the rain-drop ploughs.

How, See, And: the words of comment and connection opening the first three have no equivalent in the last.

That these are imagistic triumphs less finally found in his other poems reminds us that Hardy reaches a modern audience from a more distant and native-English poetic past than found expression in the Symbolist and Imagist movements themselves. That this kind of final irreducibility has to be visibly worked towards *within* poems nevertheless reveals the pressure of Hardy's individual experience against the forms of the older discursive-descriptive tradition. Like the existentialist mood of so much of his work, it gives him a mediating power between two different literary climates. This mediation is part of his significance, and of what we mean by tradition as a 'handing on' in the first place. The imagistic effects that most obviously appeal to us cannot be isolated from a tissue of connections – personal, social, and stylistic – out of which they grew and which also needs, elsewhere, different kinds of expression. The survival in his poetry of the norm of 'a man speaking to men' is not to be compromised.

More fully within that norm, different kinds of endings from those we have just looked at can appear simply undistinguished. But though refusing to be 'distinguished' or detached, remaining within the broader narrative-meditative style of what leads up to them, they too can create effects beyond comment. They can deepen, without transforming, Hardy's main idiom. That idiom might be described as a trapped, low-key sufficiency – but 'trapped' in the need for emotional and narrative integrity rather than in any technical or imaginative inadequacy. It is an idiom that suits so well Hardy's predilection for ordinary themes and subjects. Countless ordinary endings leave us with mysteries of tone, reference, and feeling that no paraphrasing account could do justice to – all the more movingly so because we cannot quite see why not. The final line of 'A Church Romance', for example, with Hardy's father 'as minstrel, ardent, young, and trim',

Bowing 'New Sabbath' or 'Mount Ephraim'.

Or the end of 'Proud Songsters' which sees those melodious birds before their birth as 'only particles of grain,/And earth, and air, and rain'. Or the refusal of 'At the Railway Station, Upway' to end by saying anything more than 'And so they went on till the train came in –/The convict, and boy with the violin'. In a suitably musical term, a greater 'flourish' would only muffle what we hear, in those poems, of the still sad music of humanity. Other examples remind us of the uncanny frisson that can come from a final image just *because*, like the rest of the poem, it refuses to swagger. In 'Lying Awake' the poet knows, without looking, that the village landscape is coming back to visibility with the slow dawn. The lightening east horizon, the thin twigs on trees, the dew-covered meadow. And finally the graveyard with its lettered gravestones; but so much more than finally –

> The names creeping out everywhere.

That line has, in miniature, the metaphysical shudder of a Stanley Spencer 'Resurrection' painting. It is already irreducible and endlessly suggestive.

The epic and mythic scope of a work like *The Dynasts* seems out of proportion to these smaller triumphs of vision over circumstance. Hardy's need to achieve the structural and philosophic completeness of *The Dynasts* had much to do with what Yeats, in a different context, called man's need not to feel helpless before the contents of his own mind. In the absence of traditional structures of thought, the modern poet has had to create others, that will make the continuance of thought possible. The cosmic vision of *The Dynasts* frames the shorter poems and their events. It does so explicitly in a poem like 'The Convergence of the Twain' on the sinking of the *Titanic*. Hardy did not have any structure of belief that could have created out of that event a 'Lycidas' or 'Wreck of the Deutschland'. However, what remains with us from 'The Convergence of the Twain' is not so much its evocation of the Immanent Will or the Spinner of the Years as the poem's powerful exposure of man's vanity. And it is the same exposure that is achieved in poems where, as is more often the case, no mythic structure is evoked to put it in perspective. Hardy's own comment on the poems of *Moments of Vision* (1917) was that they 'mortify the human sense of self-importance'. And in a journal entry of 1885 he had written that 'The business of the poet and novelist is to show the sorriness underlying the grandest things, and the grandeur underlying the sorriest things'. In this aim, the art of the poems, tracing the patterns of small accumulative events, is more importantly indebted to the realistic world of the novels than to *The Dynasts*. The concrete vision-and-world associated with the novels provided moreover a continuity of association which, over such a large number of poems, had its own myth-making possibilities.

What gathered to a greatness in the poems about the dead Emma, for example, was Hardy's ability to make the human story a poetry of place. As with so many other poems, and so much in the novels, we think of place not as background but as identity. The memory of a pair of lovers seen near Tooting Common in 'Beyond the Last Lamp' made Hardy claim that, without them, 'That lone lane does not exist'. The same thought is expressed in 'A Dream or No', written just before the 1913 revisit to Emma's places in Cornwall: 'Does there even a place like Saint-Juliot exist?'. But he knew that the reverse was also true: without those places, Emma, and the greater part of himself, did not exist. Incanting the very place-names in 'A Dream or No' begins an act of human resurrection. It is that two-way identity of place and person ('much of my life claims the spot as its key') that is recognized in the magnificent 'At Castle Boterel':

> Primaeval rocks form the road's steep border,
>   And much have they faced there, first and last,
> Of the transitory in Earth's long order;
>   But what they record in colour and cast
>   Is – that we two passed.

Heard rather than read, those last three words become 'we too passed'. It is only a verbal accident, but its truth is no more fragile than what the stanza, and the poem as a whole, actually do say: that Emma survives on Boterel Hill. But a strength of retrieval remains, because it was *places*, rather than a vaguer Nature, that gave Hardy this language for insight and feeling. Those places grow to significance some- where between reality and imagination, like the mixed real and fictional place-names on a map of 'Wessex'. Or like myth, as long as we remember that the excitement of first meeting Emma – 'When I Set Out for Lyonnesse', 'She Opened the Door of the West to Me' – needed the literal places of that 'West' (Cornwall, with its 'cliff-side clashings') more than any Arthurian romance of 'Lyonnesse' to release its meaning. That marvellous element of celebration in the midst of elegy is one of the reasons why it seems so inad- equate to call Hardy a pessimist. The finest flowering of that language of place as a language of imagination and identity (finally irreducible, 'facing round about me everywhere') is 'After a Journey'.

But we shall end with a more modest poem. Hardy's view of Emma reminds us of Browning's concept of 'elective affinities' – that a unique partner awaits each person. 'A man was drawing near to me': the dread irony is that it was only after Emma's death that Hardy could fully imagine this human version of the convergence of the twain. Yet, thus newly imagined, Emma's ghost re-enacts the 'awaiting'. In Browning's 'Love in a Life' the search for that unique partner prefigures the search for a dead one, and parallels the language of elegy, even as it makes 'room after room' an everywhere of expected discovery –

Next time, herself! – not the trouble behind her
Left in the curtain, the couch's perfume!
As she brushed it, the cornice-wreath blossomed anew.

Rooms, too, are places. In 'The Walk' Hardy makes us under- stand the interpenetration not only of place and person, but of place and place:

I walked up there to-day
Just in the former way;
Surveyed around
The familiar ground

By myself again:
What difference, then?
Only that underlying sense
Of the look of a room on returning thence.

The double exposure – a changed room 'underlying' a changed landscape – is finely done. The fineness lies in linking the actually private with that which can be only allegedly so. And it is a suitably domesticating insight on which to end. It reminds us of so much in Hardy's poetry that is strong because it respects 'not what the loud have spoken but what the mute have thought'.

January 1982   Walford Davies

Note on Arrangement

No strictly chronological arrangement of Hardy's poems is possible. Because of the relative consistency of his styles and preoccupations this is no great disadvantage. Hardy himself was conscious of only one danger in thus having 'poems perhaps years apart in the making . . . facing each other': the danger that those 'of a satirical and humorous intention', in following others 'in graver voice', might be read as 'misfires'. On this score he said he had to trust to the reader's 'right note-catching' to register the variety of tones ('Apology' to *Late Lyrics and Earlier*).

The present selection similarly mixes poems of different dates and tones. It groups them, however, under eight mainly thematic headings. Hardy agreed with the *Edinburgh Review* that even formal categories (lyrics, ballads, narratives etc.) are not watertight: 'The division into separate groups is frequently a question of the preponderance, not of the exclusive possession, of certain aesthetic elements' (*Life*, 359). The convenience of the present arrangement, allowing poems to come together first of all according to their main emphasis, does not remove that sense also of the seeping inter-relationship of different poems across boundaries.

Select Bibliography

TEXT
Thomas Hardy: The Complete Poems, ed. J. Gibson, 1976.

BIOGRAPHY AND AUTOBIOGRAPHY
The Life of Thomas Hardy 1840–1928 by F. E. Hardy, 1962. Originally 2 vols., 1928 and 1930. Written mostly by the poet himself.
Some Recollections by Emma Hardy, ed. E. Hardy and R. Gittings, 1961.
Young Thomas Hardy and *The Older Hardy* by R. Gittings, 1975 and 1978.
Thomas Hardy: A Biography by M. Millgate, 1982.

BIBLIOGRAPHY
Thomas Hardy: A Bibliographical Study by R. L. Purdy, 1954.
Thomas Hardy: An Annotated Bibliography of Writings about Him [to 1968] by H. E. Gerber and W. E. Davis, 1973.

HANDBOOKS
The Poetry of Thomas Hardy: A Handbook and Commentary by J. O. Bailey, 1970.
A Commentary on the Poems of Thomas Hardy by F. B. Pinion, 1976.

CRITICAL STUDIES
D. Brown, *Thomas Hardy*, 1954.
S. Hynes, *The Pattern of Hardy's Poetry*, 1961.
R. Morrell, *Thomas Hardy: The Will and the Way*, 1965.
K. Marsden, *The Poems of Thomas Hardy*, 1969.
D. Davie, *Thomas Hardy and British Poetry*, 1973.
T. Paulin, *Thomas Hardy: The Poetry of Perception*, 1975.
J. Bayley, *An Essay on Hardy*, 1978.

I The Conditions

Childhood among the Ferns

I SAT one sprinkling day upon the lea,
Where tall-stemmed ferns spread out luxuriantly,
And nothing but those tall ferns sheltered me.

The rain gained strength, and damped each lopping frond,
Ran down their stalks beside me and beyond,
And shaped slow-creeping rivulets as I conned,

With pride, my spray-roofed house. And though anon
Some drops pierced its green rafters, I sat on,
Making pretence I was not rained upon.

The sun then burst, and brought forth a sweet breath
From the limp ferns as they dried underneath:
I said: 'I could live on here thus till death;'

And queried in the green rays as I sate:
'Why should I have to grow to man's estate,
And this afar-noised World perambulate?'

Afternoon Service at Mellstock

(Circa 1850)

ON afternoons of drowsy calm
    We stood in the panelled pew,
Singing one-voiced a Tate-and-Brady psalm
    To the tune of 'Cambridge New'.

We watched the elms, we watched the rooks,
    The clouds upon the breeze,
Between the whiles of glancing at our books,
    And swaying like the trees.

So mindless were those outpourings! –
Though I am not aware
That I have gained by subtle thought on things
Since we stood psalming there.

To an Unborn Pauper Child

I

BREATHE not, hid Heart: cease silently,
And though thy birth-hour beckons thee,
      Sleep the long sleep:
      The Doomsters heap
Travails and teens around us here,
And Time-wraiths turn our songsingings to fear.

II

Hark, how the peoples surge and sigh,
And laughters fail, and greetings die:
      Hopes dwindle; yea,
      Faiths waste away,
Affections and enthusiasms numb;
Thou canst not mend these things if thou dost come.

III

Had I the ear of wombèd souls
Ere their terrestrial chart unrolls,
      And thou wert free
      To cease, or be,
Then would I tell thee all I know,
And put it to thee: Wilt thou take Life so?

IV

Vain vow! No hint of mine may hence
To theeward fly: to thy locked sense
      Explain none can
      Life's pending plan:

Thou wilt thy ignorant entry make
Though skies spout fire and blood and nations quake.

V

Fain would I, dear, find some shut plot
Of earth's wide wold for thee, where not
  One tear, one qualm,
  Should break the calm.
But I am weak as thou and bare;
No man can change the common lot to rare.

VI

Must come and bide. And such are we –
Unreasoning, sanguine, visionary –
  That I can hope
  Health, love, friends, scope
In full for thee; can dream thou'lt find
Joys seldom yet attained by humankind!

The Subalterns

I

'POOR wanderer,' said the leaden sky,
  'I fain would lighten thee,
But there are laws in force on high
  Which say it must not be.'

II

– 'I would not freeze thee, shorn one,' cried
  The North, 'knew I but how
To warm my breath, to slack my stride;
  But I am ruled as thou.'

III

– 'To-morrow I attack thee, wight,'
  Said Sickness. 'Yet I swear

I bear thy little ark no spite,
    But am bid enter there.'

IV

— 'Come hither, Son,' I heard Death say;
    'I did not will a grave
Should end thy pilgrimage to-day,
    But I, too, am a slave!'

V

We smiled upon each other then,
    And life to me had less
Of that fell look it wore ere when
    They owned their passiveness.

Discouragement

To see the Mother, naturing Nature, stand
All racked and wrung by her unfaithful lord,
Her hopes dismayed by his defiling hand,
Her passioned plans for bloom and beauty marred.

Where she would mint a perfect mould, an ill;
Where she would don divinest hues, a stain,
Over her purposed genial hour a chill,
Upon her charm of flawless flesh a blain:

Her loves dependent on a feature's trim,
A whole life's circumstance on hap of birth,
A soul's direction on a body's whim,
Eternal Heaven upon a day of Earth,
Is frost to flower of heroism and worth,
And fosterer of visions ghast and grim.

Westbourne Park Villas, 1863–7
(From old MS.)

Revulsion

THOUGH I waste watches framing words to fetter
Some unknown spirit to mine in clasp and kiss,
Out of the night there looms a sense 'twere better
To fail obtaining whom one fails to miss.

For winning love we win the risk of losing,
And losing love is as one's life were riven;
It cuts like contumely and keen ill-using
To cede what was superfluously given.

Let me then never feel the fateful thrilling
That devastates the love-worn wooer's frame,
The hot ado of fevered hopes, the chilling
That agonizes disappointed aim!
So may I live no junctive law fulfilling,
And my heart's table bear no woman's name.

1866

She, to Him I

WHEN you shall see me in the toils of Time,
My lauded beauties carried off from me,
My eyes no longer stars as in their prime,
My name forgot of Maiden Fair and Free;

When, in your being, heart concedes to mind,
And judgment, though you scarce its process know,
Recalls the excellencies I once enshrined,
And you are irked that they have withered so:

Remembering mine the loss is, not the blame,
That Sportsman Time but rears his brood to kill,
Knowing me in my soul the very same —
One who would die to spare you touch of ill! —
Will you not grant to old affection's claim
The hand of friendship down Life's sunless hill?

1866

She, to Him III

I WILL be faithful to thee; aye, I will!
And Death shall choose me with a wondering eye
That he did not discern and domicile
One his by right ever since that last Good-bye!

I have no care for friends, or kin, or prime
Of manhood who deal gently with me here;
Amid the happy people of my time
Who work their love's fulfilment, I appear

Numb as a vane that cankers on its point,
True to the wind that kissed ere canker came:
Despised by souls of Now, who would disjoint
The mind from memory, making Life all aim,

My old dexterities in witchery gone,
And nothing left for Love to look upon.

1866

Her Dilemma

(In —— Church)

THE two were silent in a sunless church,
Whose mildewed walls, uneven paving-stones,
And wasted carvings passed antique research;
And nothing broke the clock's dull monotones.

Leaning against a wormy poppy-head,
So wan and worn that he could scarcely stand,
– For he was soon to die, – he softly said,
'Tell me you love me!' – holding long her hand.

She would have given a world to breathe 'yes' truly,
So much his life seemed hanging on her mind,
And hence she lied, her heart persuaded throughly
'Twas worth her soul to be a moment kind.

But the sad need thereof, his nearing death,
So mocked humanity that she shamed to prize
A world conditioned thus, or care for breath
Where Nature such dilemmas could devise.

1866

In Tenebris I

'Percussus sum sicut fœnum, et aruit cor meum.' – Ps. CI

WINTERTIME nighs;
But my bereavement-pain
It cannot bring again:
    Twice no one dies.

Flower-petals flee;
But, since it once hath been,
No more that severing scene
    Can harrow me.

Birds faint in dread:
I shall not lose old strength
In the lone frost's black length:
    Strength long since fled!

Leaves freeze to dun;
But friends can not turn cold
This season as of old
    For him with none.

Tempests may scath;
But love can not make smart
Again this year his heart
    Who no heart hath.

Black is night's cope;
But death will not appal
One who, past doubtings all,
    Waits in unhope.

In Tenebris II

'Considerabam ad dexteram, et videbam; et non erat qui
    cognosceret me.... non est qui requirat animam meam.' – Ps. CXLI

WHEN the clouds' swoln bosoms echo back the shouts of the
        many and strong
That things are all as they best may be, save a few to be right
        ere long,
And my eyes have not the vision in them to discern what to
        these is so clear,
The blot seems straightway in me alone; one better he were
        not here.

The stout upstanders say, All's well with us: ruers have
        nought to rue!
And what the potent say so oft, can it fail to be somewhat
        true?
Breezily go they, breezily come; their dust smokes around
        their career,
Till I think I am one born out of due time, who has no calling
        here.

Their dawns bring lusty joys, it seems; their evenings all that
        is sweet;
Our times are blessed times, they cry: Life shapes it as is most
        meet,
And nothing is much the matter; there are many smiles to a
        tear;
Then what is the matter is I, I say. Why should such an one be
        here? . . .

Let him in whose ears the low-voiced Best is killed by the
        clash of the First,
Who holds that if way to the Better there be, it exacts a full
        look at the Worst,
Who feels that delight is a delicate growth cramped by
        crookedness, custom, and fear,
Get him up and be gone as one shaped awry; he disturbs
        the order here.

1895–96

In Tenebris III

'Heu mihi, quia incolatus meus prolongatus est! Habitavi cum
habitantibus Cedar. Multum incola fuit anima mea.' – Ps. cxix

THERE have been times when I well might have passed and
    the ending have come –
Points in my path when the dark might have stolen on me,
    artless, unrueing –
Ere I had learnt that the world was a welter of futile doing:
Such had been times when I well might have passed, and the
    ending have come!

Say, on the noon when the half-sunny hours told that April
    was nigh,
And I upgathered and cast forth the snow from the
    crocus-border,
Fashioned and furbished the soil into a summer-seeming
    order,
Glowing in gladsome faith that I quickened the year thereby.

Or on that loneliest of eves when afar and benighted we
    stood,
She who upheld me and I, in the midmost of Egdon together,
Confident I in her watching and ward through the
    blackening heather,
Deeming her matchless in might and with measureless scope
    endued.

Or on that winter-wild night when, reclined by the
    chimney-nook quoin,
Slowly a drowse overgat me, the smallest and feeblest of folk
    there,
Weak from my baptism of pain; when at times and anon I
    awoke there –
Heard of a world wheeling on, with no listing or longing to
    join.

Even then! while unweeting that vision could vex or that
    knowledge could numb,

That sweets to the mouth in the belly are bitter, and tart, and
    untoward,
Then, on some dim-coloured scene should my briefly raised
    curtain have lowered,
Then might the Voice that is law have said 'Cease!' and the
    ending have come.

1896

A Wasted Illness

THROUGH vaults of pain,
Enribbed and wrought with groins of ghastliness,
I passed, and garish spectres moved my brain
        To dire distress.

        And hammerings,
And quakes, and shoots, and stifling hotness, blent
With webby waxing things and waning things
        As on I went.

        'Where lies the end
To this foul way?' I asked with weakening breath.
Thereon ahead I saw a door extend –
        The door to Death.

        It loomed more clear:
'At last!' I cried. 'The all-delivering door!'
And then, I knew not how, it grew less near
        Than theretofore.

        And back slid I
Along the galleries by which I came,
And tediously the day returned, and sky,
        And life – the same.

        And all was well:
Old circumstance resumed its former show,
And on my head the dews of comfort fell
        As ere my woe.

I roam anew,
Scarce conscious of my late distress. . . . And yet
Those backward steps to strength I cannot view
    Without regret.

    For that dire train
Of waxing shapes and waning, passed before,
And those grim chambers, must be ranged again
    To reach that door.

The Dead Man Walking

THEY hail me as one living,
    But don't they know
That I have died of late years,
    Untombed although?

I am but a shape that stands here,
    A pulseless mould,
A pale past picture, screening
    Ashes gone cold.

Not at a minute's warning,
    Not in a loud hour,
For me ceased Time's enchantments
    In hall and bower.

There was no tragic transit,
    No catch of breath,
When silent seasons inched me
    On to this death. . . .

  – A Troubadour-youth I rambled
    With Life for lyre,
The beats of being raging
    In me like fire.

But when I practised eyeing
    The goal of men,
It iced me, and I perished
    A little then.

When passed my friend, my kinsfolk,
　　Through the Last Door,
And left me standing bleakly,
　　I died yet more;

And when my Love's heart kindled
　　In hate of me,
Wherefore I knew not, died I
　　One more degree.

And if when I died fully
　　I cannot say,
And changed into the corpse-thing
　　I am to-day;

Yet is it that, though whiling
　　The time somehow
In walking, talking, smiling,
　　I live not now.

The Something that Saved Him

　　IT was when
Whirls of thick waters laved me
　　Again and again,
That something arose and saved me;
　　Yea, it was then.

　　In that day
Unseeing the azure went I
　　On my way,
And to white winter bent I,
　　Knowing no May.

　　Reft of renown,
Under the night clouds beating
　　Up and down,
In my needfulness greeting
　　Cit and clown.

Long there had been
Much of a murky colour
    In the scene,
Dull prospects meeting duller;
    Nought between.

Last, there loomed
A closing-in blind alley,
    Though there boomed
A feeble summons to rally
    Where it gloomed.

The clock rang;
The hour brought a hand to deliver;
    I upsprang,
And looked back at den, ditch and river,
    And sang.

Yell'ham-Wood's Story

COOMB-FIRTREES say that Life is a moan,
    And Clyffe-hill Clump says 'Yea!'
But Yell'ham says a thing of its own:
        It's not 'Gray, gray
        Is Life alway!'
        That Yell'ham says,
    Nor that Life is for ends unknown.

It says that Life would signify
    A thwarted purposing:
That we come to live, and are called to die.
        Yes, that's the thing
        In fall, in spring,
        That Yell'ham says: —
    'Life offers — to deny!'

1902

Hap

IF but some vengeful god would call to me
From up the sky, and laugh: 'Thou suffering thing,
Know that thy sorrow is my ecstasy,
That thy love's loss is my hate's profiting!'

Then would I bear it, clench myself, and die,
Steeled by the sense of ire unmerited;
Half-eased in that a Powerfuller than I
Had willed and meted me the tears I shed.

But not so. How arrives it joy lies slain,
And why unblooms the best hope ever sown?
– Crass Casualty obstructs the sun and rain,
And dicing Time for gladness casts a moan. . . .
These purblind Doomsters had as readily strown
Blisses about my pilgrimage as pain.

1866

The Convergence of the Twain

(Lines on the loss of the 'Titanic')

I

IN a solitude of the sea
Deep from human vanity,
And the Pride of Life that planned her, stilly couches she.

II

Steel chambers, late the pyres
Of her salamandrine fires,
Cold currents thrid, and turn to rhythmic tidal lyres.

III

Over the mirrors meant
To glass the opulent
The sea-worm crawls – grotesque, slimed, dumb,
indifferent.

IV

Jewels in joy designed
To ravish the sensuous mind
Lie lightless, all their sparkles bleared and black and blind.

V

Dim moon-eyed fishes near
Gaze at the gilded gear
And query: 'What does this vaingloriousness down
here?' . . .

VI

Well: while was fashioning
This creature of cleaving wing,
The Immanent Will that stirs and urges everything

VII

Prepared a sinister mate
For her – so gaily great –
A Shape of Ice, for the time far and dissociate.

VIII

And as the smart ship grew
In stature, grace, and hue,
In shadowy silent distance grew the Iceberg too.

IX

Alien they seemed to be:
No mortal eye could see
The intimate welding of their later history,

X

Or sign that they were bent
By paths coincident
On being anon twin halves of one august event,

XI

Till the Spinner of the Years
Said 'Now!' And each one hears,
And consummation comes, and jars two hemispheres.

God-Forgotten

I TOWERED far, and lo! I stood within
The presence of the Lord Most High,
Sent thither by the sons of Earth, to win
    Some answer to their cry.

– 'The Earth, sayest thou? The Human race?
By Me created? Sad its lot?
Nay: I have no remembrance of such place:
    Such world I fashioned not.' –

– 'O Lord, forgive me when I say
Thou spakest the word that made it all.' –
'The Earth of men – let me bethink me. . . . Yea!
    I dimly do recall

'Some tiny sphere I built long back
(Mid millions of such shapes of mine)
So named . . . It perished, surely – not a wrack
    Remaining, or a sign?

'It lost my interest from the first,
My aims therefore succeeding ill;
Haply it died of doing as it durst?' –
    'Lord, it existeth still.' –

'Dark, then, its life! For not a cry
    Of aught it bears do I now hear;
Of its own act the threads were snapt whereby
    Its plaints had reached mine ear.

'It used to ask for gifts of good,
    Till came its severance, self-entailed,
When sudden silence on that side ensued,
    And has till now prevailed.

'All other orbs have kept in touch;
    Their voicings reach me speedily:
Thy people took upon them overmuch
    In sundering them from me!

'And it is strange – though sad enough –
    Earth's race should think that one whose call
Frames, daily, shining spheres of flawless stuff
    Must heed their tainted ball! . . .

'But sayest it is by pangs distraught,
    And strife, and silent suffering? –
Sore grieved am I that injury should be wrought
    Even on so poor a thing!

'Thou shouldst have learnt that *Not to Mend*
    For Me could mean but *Not to Know*:
Hence, Messengers! and straightway put an end
    To what men undergo.' . . .

    Homing at dawn, I thought to see
    One of the Messengers standing by.
– Oh, childish thought! . . . Yet often it comes to me
    When trouble hovers nigh.

A Plaint to Man

WHEN you slowly emerged from the den of Time,
And gained percipience as you grew,
And fleshed you fair out of shapeless slime,

Wherefore, O Man, did there come to you
The unhappy need of creating me –
A form like your own – for praying to?

My virtue, power, utility,
Within my maker must all abide,
Since none in myself can ever be,

One thin as a phasm on a lantern-slide
Shown forth in the dark upon some dim sheet,
And by none but its showman vivified.

'Such a forced device,' you may say, 'is meet
For easing a loaded heart at whiles:
Man needs to conceive of a mercy-seat

Somewhere above the gloomy aisles
Of this wailful world, or he could not bear
The irk no local hope beguiles.'

– But since I was framed in your first despair
The doing without me has had no play
In the minds of men when shadows scare;

And now that I dwindle day by day
Beneath the deicide eyes of seers
In a light that will not let me stay,

And to-morrow the whole of me disappears,
The truth should be told, and the fact be faced
That had best been faced in earlier years:

The fact of life with dependence placed
On the human heart's resource alone,
In brotherhood bonded close and graced

With loving-kindness fully blown,
And visioned help unsought, unknown.

1909–10

A Cathedral Façade at Midnight

ALONG the sculptures of the western wall
    I watched the moonlight creeping:
It moved as if it hardly moved at all,
    Inch by inch thinly peeping
Round on the pious figures of freestone, brought
And poised there when the Universe was wrought
To serve its centre, Earth, in mankind's thought,

The lunar look skimmed scantly toe, breast, arm,
    Then edged on slowly, slightly,
To shoulder, hand, face; till each austere form
    Was blanched its whole length brightly
Of prophet, king, queen, cardinal in state,
That dead men's tools had striven to simulate;
And the stiff images stood irradiate.

A frail moan from the martyred saints there set
    Mid others of the erection
Against the breeze, seemed sighings of regret
    At the ancient faith's rejection
Under the sure, unhasting, steady stress
Of Reason's movement, making meaningless
The coded creeds of old-time godliness.

Mute Opinion

I

I TRAVERSED a dominion
Whose spokesmen spake out strong
Their purpose and opinion
Through pulpit, press, and song.
I scarce had means to note there
A large-eyed few, and dumb,
Who thought not as those thought there
That stirred the heat and hum.

II

When, grown a Shade, beholding
That land in lifetime trode,
To learn if its unfolding
Fulfilled its clamoured code,
I saw, in web unbroken,
Its history outwrought
Not as the loud had spoken,
But as the mute had thought.

Drummer Hodge

I

THEY throw in Drummer Hodge, to rest
        Uncoffined – just as found:
His landmark is a kopje-crest
        That breaks the veldt around;
And foreign constellations west
        Each night above his mound.

II

Young Hodge the Drummer never knew –
        Fresh from his Wessex home –
The meaning of the broad Karoo,
        The Bush, the dusty loam,
And why uprose to nightly view
        Strange stars amid the gloam.

III

Yet portion of that unknown plain
        Will Hodge for ever be;
His homely Northern breast and brain
        Grow to some Southern tree,
And strange-eyed constellations reign
        His stars eternally.

The Souls of the Slain

I

THE thick lids of Night closed upon me
　　Alone at the Bill
　　Of the Isle by the Race[1] –
Many-caverned, bald, wrinkled of face –
And with darkness and silence the spirit was on me
　　To brood and be still.

II

No wind fanned the flats of the ocean,
　　Or promontory sides,
　　Or the ooze by the strand,
Or the bent-bearded slope of the land,
Whose base took its rest amid everlong motion
　　Of criss-crossing tides.

III

Soon from out of the Southward seemed nearing
　　A whirr, as of wings
　　Waved by mighty-vanned flies,
Or by night-moths of measureless size,
And in softness and smoothness well-nigh beyond hearing
　　Of corporal things.

IV

And they bore to the bluff, and alighted –
　　A dim-discerned train
　　Of sprites without mould,
Frameless souls none might touch or might hold –
On the ledge by the turreted lantern, far-sighted
　　By men of the main.

[1] The 'Race' is the turbulent sea-area off the Bill of Portland, where
contrary tides meet.

V

And I heard them say 'Home!' and I knew them
    For souls of the felled
    On the earth's nether bord
Under Capricorn, whither they'd warred,
And I neared in my awe, and gave heedfulness to them
    With breathings inheld.

VI

Then, it seemed, there approached from the northward
    A senior soul-flame
    Of the like filmy hue:
And he met them and spake: 'Is it you,
O my men?' Said they, 'Aye! We bear homeward and
      hearthward
    To feast on our fame!'

VII

'I've flown there before you,' he said then:
    'Your households are well;
    But – your kin linger less
On your glory and war-mightiness
Than on dearer things.' – 'Dearer?' cried these from the
      dead then,
    'Of what do they tell?'

VIII

'Some mothers muse sadly, and murmur
    Your doings as boys –
    Recall the quaint ways
Of your babyhood's innocent days.
Some pray that, ere dying, your faith had grown firmer,
    And higher your joys.

IX

'A father broods: "Would I had set him
    To some humble trade,
    And so slacked his high fire,
And his passionate martial desire;

And told him no stories to woo him and whet him
    To this dire crusade!'' '

X

  'And, General, how hold out our sweethearts,
    Sworn loyal as doves?'
    – 'Many mourn; many think
  It is not unattractive to prink
Them in sables for heroes. Some fickle and fleet hearts
    Have found them new loves.'

XI

  'And our wives?' quoth another resignedly,
    'Dwell they on our deeds?'
    – 'Deeds of home; that live yet
  Fresh as new – deeds of fondness or fret;
Ancient words that were kindly expressed or unkindly,
    These, these have their heeds.'

XII

  – 'Alas! then it seems that our glory
    Weighs less in their thought
    Than our old homely acts,
  And the long-ago commonplace facts
Of our lives – held by us as scarce part of our story,
    And rated as nought!'

XIII

  Then bitterly some: 'Was it wise now
    To raise the tomb-door
    For such knowledge? Away!'
  But the rest: 'Fame we prized till to-day;
Yet that hearts keep us green for old kindness we prize now
    A thousand times more!'

XIV

  Thus speaking, the trooped apparitions
    Began to disband
    And resolve them in two:
  Those whose record was lovely and true

Bore to northward for home: those of bitter traditions
      Again left the land,

XV

  And, towering to seaward in legions,
      They paused at a spot
      Overbending the Race –
  That engulphing, ghast, sinister place –
Whither headlong they plunged, to the fathomless regions
      Of myriads forgot.

XVI

  And the spirits of those who were homing
      Passed on, rushingly,
      Like the Pentecost Wind;
  And the whirr of their wayfaring thinned
And surceased on the sky, and but left in the gloaming
      Sea-mutterings and me.

December 1899

The Man He Killed

    'HAD he and I but met
      By some old ancient inn,
  We should have sat us down to wet
      Right many a nipperkin!

    'But ranged as infantry,
      And staring face to face,
  I shot at him as he at me,
      And killed him in his place.

    'I shot him dead because –
      Because he was my foe,
  Just so: my foe of course he was;
      That's clear enough; although

'He thought he'd 'list, perhaps,
　　Off-hand like – just as I –
Was out of work – had sold his traps –
　　No other reason why.

'Yes; quaint and curious war is!
　　You shoot a fellow down
You'd treat if met where any bar is,
　　Or help to half-a-crown.'

1902

Channel Firing

THAT night your great guns, unawares,
Shook all our coffins as we lay,
And broke the chancel window-squares,
We thought it was the Judgment-day

And sat upright. While drearisome
Arose the howl of wakened hounds:
The mouse let fall the altar-crumb,
The worms drew back into the mounds,

The glebe cow drooled. Till God called, 'No;
It's gunnery practice out at sea
Just as before you went below;
The world is as it used to be:

'All nations striving strong to make
Red war yet redder. Mad as hatters
They do no more for Christés sake
Than you who are helpless in such matters.

'That this is not the judgment-hour
For some of them's a blessed thing,
For if it were they'd have to scour
Hell's floor for so much threatening. . . .

'Ha, ha. It will be warmer when
I blow the trumpet (if indeed
I ever do; for you are men,
And rest eternal sorely need).'

So down we lay again. 'I wonder,
Will the world ever saner be,'
Said one, 'than when He sent us under
In our indifferent century!'

And many a skeleton shook his head.
'Instead of preaching forty year,'
My neighbour Parson Thirdly said,
'I wish I had stuck to pipes and beer.'

Again the guns disturbed the hour,
Roaring their readiness to avenge,
As far inland as Stourton Tower,
And Camelot, and starlit Stonehenge.

April 1914

In Time of 'The Breaking of Nations'[1]

I

ONLY a man harrowing clods
    In a slow silent walk
With an old horse that stumbles and nods
    Half asleep as they stalk.

II

Only thin smoke without flame
    From the heaps of couch-grass;
Yet this will go onward the same
    Though Dynasties pass.

[1] Jer., LI 20.

III

Yonder a maid and her wight
   Come whispering by:
War's annals will cloud into night
   Ere their story die.

1915

'I Met a Man'

I MET a man when night was nigh,
   Who said, with shining face and eye
Like Moses' after Sinai: –

'I have seen the Moulder of Monarchies,
   Realms, peoples, plains and hills,
Sitting upon the sunlit seas! –
And, as He sat, soliloquies
Fell from Him like an antiphonic breeze
   That pricks the waves to thrills.

'Meseemed that of the maimed and dead
   Mown down upon the globe, –
Their plenteous blooms of promise shed
Ere fruiting-time – His words were said,
Sitting against the western web of red
   Wrapt in His crimson robe.

'And I could catch them now and then:
   – "Why let these gambling clans
Of human Cockers, pit liege men
From mart and city, dale and glen,
In death-mains, but to swell and swell again
   Their swollen All-Empery plans,

' "When a mere nod (if my malign
   Compeer but passive keep)
Would mend that old mistake of mine
I made with Saul, and ever consign

All Lords of War whose sanctuaries enshrine
    Liberticide, to sleep?

‘ "With violence the lands are spread
    Even as in Israel's day,
And it repenteth me I bred
Chartered armipotents lust-led
To feuds. . . . Yea, grieves my heart, as then I said,
    To see their evil way!"

– 'The utterance grew, and flapped like flame,
    And further speech I feared;
But no Celestial tongued acclaim,
And no huzzas from earthlings came,
And the heavens mutely masked as 'twere in shame
    Till daylight disappeared.'

Thus ended he as night rode high –
The man of shining face and eye,
Like Moses' after Sinai.

1916

A New Year's Eve in War Time

I

PHANTASMAL fears,
And the flap of the flame,
And the throb of the clock,
And a loosened slate,
And the blind night's drone,
Which tiredly the spectral pines intone!

II

And the blood in my ears
Strumming always the same,
And the gable-cock
With its fitful grate,
And myself, alone.

III

The twelfth hour nears
Hand-hid, as in shame;
I undo the lock,
And listen, and wait
For the Young Unknown.

IV

In the dark there careers –
As if Death astride came
To numb all with his knock –
A horse at mad rate
Over rut and stone.

V

No figure appears,
No call of my name,
No sound but 'Tic-toc'
Without check. Past the gate
It clatters – is gone.

VI

What rider it bears
There is none to proclaim;
And the Old Year has struck,
And, scarce animate,
The New makes moan.

VII

Maybe that 'More Tears! –
More Famine and Flame –
More Severance and Shock!'
Is the order from Fate
That the Rider speeds on
To pale Europe; and tiredly the pines intone.

1915–1916

'I Looked Up from My Writing'

I LOOKED up from my writing,
   And gave a start to see,
As if rapt in my inditing,
   The moon's full gaze on me.

Her meditative misty head
   Was spectral in its air,
And I involuntarily said,
   'What are you doing there?'

'Oh, I've been scanning pond and hole
   And waterway hereabout
For the body of one with a sunken soul
   Who has put his life-light out.

'Did you hear his frenzied tattle?
   It was sorrow for his son
Who is slain in brutish battle,
   Though he has injured none.

'And now I am curious to look
   Into the blinkered mind
Of one who wants to write a book
   In a world of such a kind.'

Her temper overwrought me,
   And I edged to shun her view,
For I felt assured she thought me
   One who should drown him too.

According to the Mighty Working

I

WHEN moiling seems at cease
    In the vague void of night-time,
    And heaven's wide roomage stormless
    Between the dusk and light-time,
    And fear at last is formless,
We call the allurement Peace.

II

Peace, this hid riot, Change,
    This revel of quick-cued mumming,
    This never truly being,
    This evermore becoming,
    This spinner's wheel onfleeing
Outside perception's range.

    1917

Christmas: 1924

'PEACE upon earth!' was said. We sing it,
And pay a million priests to bring it.
After two thousand years of mass
We've got as far as poison-gas.

    1924

The Respectable Burgher

On 'The Higher Criticism'

SINCE Reverend Doctors now declare
That clerks and people must prepare
To doubt if Adam ever were;
To hold the flood a local scare;
To argue, though the stolid stare,
That everything had happened ere
The prophets to its happening sware;
That David was no giant-slayer,
Nor one to call a God-obeyer
In certain details we could spare,
But rather was a debonair
Shrewd bandit, skilled as banjo-player:
That Solomon sang the fleshly Fair,
And gave the Church no thought whate'er,
That Esther with her royal wear,
And Mordecai, the son of Jair,
And Joshua's triumphs, Job's despair,
And Balaam's ass's bitter blare;
Nebuchadnezzar's furnace-flare,
And Daniel and the den affair,
And other stories rich and rare,
Were writ to make old doctrine wear
Something of a romantic air:
That the Nain widow's only heir,
And Lazarus with cadaverous glare
(As done in oils by Piombo's care)
Did not return from Sheol's lair:
That Jael set a fiendish snare,
That Pontius Pilate acted square,
That never a sword cut Malchus' ear;
And (but for shame I must forbear)
That —— —— did not reappear! . . .
– Since thus they hint, nor turn a hair,
All churchgoing will I forswear,
And sit on Sundays in my chair,
And read that moderate man Voltaire.

Yuletide in a Younger World

WE believed in highdays then,
    And could glimpse at night
      On Christmas Eve
Imminent oncomings of radiant revel –
    Doings of delight:–
    Now we have no such sight.

  We had eyes for phantoms then,
    And at bridge or stile
      On Christmas Eve
Clear beheld those countless ones who had crossed it
    Cross again in file: –
    Such has ceased longwhile!

  We liked divination then,
    And, as they homeward wound
      On Christmas Eve,
We could read men's dreams within them spinning
    Even as wheels spin round: –
    Now we are blinker-bound.

  We heard still small voices then,
    And, in the dim serene
      Of Christmas Eve,
Caught the far-time tones of fire-filled prophets
    Long on earth unseen. . . .
    – Can such ever have been?

A Sign-Seeker

I MARK the months in liveries dank and dry,
  The noontides many-shaped and hued;
  I see the nightfall shades subtrude,
And hear the monotonous hours clang negligently by.

I view the evening bonfires of the sun
  On hills where morning rains have hissed;
  The eyeless countenance of the mist
Pallidly rising when the summer droughts are done.

I have seen the lightning-blade, the leaping star,
  The cauldrons of the sea in storm,
  Have felt the earthquake's lifting arm,
And trodden where abysmal fires and snow-cones are.

I learn to prophesy the hid eclipse,
  The coming of eccentric orbs;
  To mete the dust the sky absorbs,
To weigh the sun, and fix the hour each planet dips.

I witness fellow earth-men surge and strive;
  Assemblies meet, and throb, and part;
  Death's sudden finger, sorrow's smart;
– All the vast various moils that mean a world alive.

But that I fain would wot of shuns my sense –
  Those sights of which old prophets tell,
  Those signs the general word so well
As vouchsafed their unheed, denied my long suspense.

In graveyard green, where his pale dust lies pent
  To glimpse a phantom parent, friend,
  Wearing his smile, and 'Not the end!'
Outbreathing softly: that were blest enlightenment;

Or, if a dead Love's lips, whom dreams reveal
  When midnight imps of King Decay
  Delve sly to solve me back to clay,
Should leave some print to prove her spirit-kisses real;

Or, when Earth's Frail lie bleeding of her Strong,
  If some Recorder, as in Writ,
  Near to the weary scene should flit
And drop one plume as pledge that Heaven inscrolls the
    wrong.

– There are who, rapt to heights of trancelike trust,
  These tokens claim to feel and see,
  Read radiant hints of times to be –
Of heart to heart returning after dust to dust.

Such scope is granted not to lives like mine . . .
  I have lain in dead men's beds, have walked
  The tombs of those with whom I had talked,
Called many a gone and goodly one to shape a sign,

And panted for response. But none replies;
  No warnings loom, nor whisperings
  To open out my limitings,
And Nescience mutely muses: When a man falls he lies.

The Impercipient

(At a Cathedral Service)

THAT with this bright believing band
  I have no claim to be,
That faiths by which my comrades stand
  Seem fantasies to me,
And mirage-mists their Shining Land,
  Is a strange destiny.

Why thus my soul should be consigned
  To infelicity,
Why always I must feel as blind
  To sights my brethren see,
Why joys they've found I cannot find,
  Abides a mystery.

Since heart of mine knows not that ease
  Which they know; since it be
That He who breathes All's Well to these
  Breathes no All's-Well to me,
My lack might move their sympathies
  And Christian charity!

I am like a gazer who should mark
    An inland company
Standing upfingered, with, 'Hark! hark!
    The glorious distant sea!'
And feel, 'Alas, 'tis but yon dark
    And wind-swept pine to me!'

Yet I would bear my shortcomings
    With meet tranquillity,
But for the charge that blessed things
    I'd liefer not have be.
O, doth a bird deprived of wings
    Go earth-bound wilfully!

    .   .   .

Enough. As yet disquiet clings
    About us. Rest shall we.

The Oxen

CHRISTMAS EVE, and twelve of the clock.
    'Now they are all on their knees,'
An elder said as we sat in a flock
    By the embers in hearthside ease.

We pictured the meek mild creatures where
    They dwelt in their strawy pen,
Nor did it occur to one of us there
    To doubt they were kneeling then.

So fair a fancy few would weave
    In these years! Yet, I feel,
If someone said on Christmas Eve,
    'Come; see the oxen kneel

'In the lonely barton by yonder coomb
    Our childhood used to know,'
I should go with him in the gloom,
    Hoping it might be so.

1915

A Drizzling Easter Morning

AND he is risen? Well, be it so. . . .
And still the pensive lands complain,
And dead men wait as long ago,
As if, much doubting, they would know
What they are ransomed from, before
They pass again their sheltering door.

I stand amid them in the rain,
While blusters vex the yew and vane;
And on the road the weary wain
Plods forward, laden heavily;
And toilers with their aches are fain
For endless rest – though risen is he.

'I Look Into My Glass'

I LOOK into my glass,
And view my wasting skin,
And say, 'Would God it came to pass
My heart had shrunk as thin!'

For then, I, undistrest
By hearts grown cold to me,
Could lonely wait my endless rest
With equanimity.

But Time, to make me grieve,
Part steals, lets part abide;
And shakes this fragile frame at eve
With throbbings of noontide.

He Abjures Love

AT last I put off love,
   For twice ten years
The daysman of my thought,
   And hope, and doing;
Being ashamed thereof,
   And faint of fears
And desolations, wrought
   In his pursuing,

Since first in youthtime those
   Disquietings
That heart-enslavement brings
   To hale and hoary,
Became my housefellows,
   And, fool and blind,
I turned from kith and kind
   To give him glory.

I was as children be
   Who have no care;
I did not shrink or sigh,
   I did not sicken;
But lo, Love beckoned me,
   And I was bare,
And poor, and starved, and dry,
   And fever-stricken.

Too many times ablaze
   With fatuous fires,
Enkindled by his wiles
   To new embraces,
Did I, by wilful ways
   And baseless ires,
Return the anxious smiles
   Of friendly faces.

No more will now rate I
   The common rare,
The midnight drizzle dew,
   The gray hour golden,

The wind a yearning cry,
   The faulty fair,
Things dreamt, of comelier hue
   Than things beholden! . . .

– I speak as one who plumbs
   Life's dim profound,
One who at length can sound
   Clear views and certain.
But – after love what comes?
   A scene that lours,
A few sad vacant hours,
   And then, the Curtain.

   1883

Drinking Song

ONCE on a time when thought began
   Lived Thales: he
   Was said to see
Vast truths that mortals seldom can;
   It seems without
   A moment's doubt
That everything was made for man.

Chorus

Fill full your cups: feel no distress
That thoughts so great should now be less!

Earth mid the sky stood firm and flat,
   He held, till came
   A sage by name
Copernicus, and righted that.
   We trod, he told,
   A globe that rolled
Around a sun it warmed it at.

Chorus

Fill full your cups: feel no distress;
'Tis only one great thought the less!

But still we held, as Time flew by
                And wit increased,
                Ours was, at least,
The only world whose rank was high:
                Till rumours flew
                From folk who knew
Of globes galore about the sky.

Chorus

Fill full your cups: feel no distress;
'Tis only one great thought the less!

And that this earth, our one estate,
                Was no prime ball,
                The best of all,
But common, mean; indeed, tenth-rate:
                And men, so proud,
                A feeble crowd,
Unworthy any special fate.

Chorus

Fill full your cups: feel no distress;
'Tis only one great thought the less!

Then rose one Hume, who could not see,
                If earth were such,
                Required were much
To prove no miracles could be:
                'Better believe
                The eyes deceive
Than that God's clockwork jolts,' said he.

Chorus

Fill full your cups: feel no distress;
'Tis only one great thought the less!

Next this strange message Darwin brings,
  (Though saying his say
  In a quiet way);
We all are one with creeping things;
  And apes and men
  Blood-brethren,
And likewise reptile forms with stings.

Chorus
  Fill full your cups: feel no distress;
  'Tis only one great thought the less!

And when this philosoph had done
  Came Doctor Cheyne:
  Speaking plain he
Proved no virgin bore a son.
  'Such tale, indeed,
  Helps not our creed,'
He said. 'A tale long known to none.'

Chorus
  Fill full your cups: feel no distress;
  'Tis only one great thought the less!

And now comes Einstein with a notion –
  Not yet quite clear
  To many here –
That there's no time, no space, no motion,
  Nor rathe nor late,
  Nor square nor straight,
But just a sort of bending-ocean.

Chorus
  Fill full your cups: feel no distress;
  'Tis only one great thought the less!

So here we are, in piteous case:
  Like butterflies
  Of many dyes
Upon an Alpine glacier's face:
  To fly and cower
  In some warm bower
Our chief concern in such a place.

Chorus

Fill full your cups: feel no distress
At all our great thoughts shrinking less:
We'll do a good deed nevertheless!

'We Are Getting to the End'

WE are getting to the end of visioning
The impossible within this universe,
Such as that better whiles may follow worse,
And that our race may mend by reasoning.

We know that even as larks in cages sing
Unthoughtful of deliverance from the curse
That holds them lifelong in a latticed hearse,
We ply spasmodically our pleasuring.

And that when nations set them to lay waste
Their neighbours' heritage by foot and horse,
And hack their pleasant plains in festering seams,
They may again, – not warely, or from taste,
But tickled mad by some demonic force. –
Yes. We are getting to the end of dreams!

Fragment

AT last I entered a long dark gallery,
   Catacomb-lined; and ranged at the side
   Were the bodies of men from far and wide
Who, motion past, were nevertheless not dead.

   'The sense of waiting here strikes strong;
Everyone's waiting, waiting, it seems to me;
   What are you waiting for so long? –
      What is to happen?' I said.

'O we are waiting for one called God,' said they,
  '(Though by some the Will, or Force, or Laws;
  And, vaguely, by some, the Ultimate Cause);
Waiting for him to see us before we are clay.
  Yes; waiting, waiting, for God *to know it*.' . . .
    'To know what?' questioned I.
'To know how things have been going on earth and
      below it:
  It is clear he must know some day.'
  I thereon asked them why.
    'Since he made us humble pioneers
    Of himself in consciousness of Life's tears,
    It needs no mighty prophecy
    To tell that what he could mindlessly show
    His creatures, he himself will know.

    'By some still close-cowled mystery
    We have reached feeling faster than he,
    But he will overtake us anon,
      If the world goes on.'

The Absolute Explains

I

  'O NO,' said It: 'her lifedoings
    Time's touch hath not destroyed:
  They lie their length, with the throbbing things
    Akin them, down the Void,
      Live, unalloyed.

II

  'Know, Time is toothless, seen all through;
    The Present, that men but see,
  Is phasmal: since in a sane purview
    All things are shaped to be
      Eternally.

III

'Your "Now" is just a gleam, a glide
    Across your gazing sense:
With me, "Past", "Future", ever abide:
    They come not, go not, whence
        They are never hence.

IV

'As one upon a dark highway,
    Plodding by lantern-light,
Finds but the reach of its frail ray
    Uncovered to his sight,
        Though mid the night

V

'The road lies all its length the same,
    Forwardly as at rear,
So, outside what you "Present" name,
    Future and Past stand sheer,
        Cognate and clear.'

VI

– Thus It: who straightway opened then
    The vista called the Past,
Wherein were seen, as fair as when
    They seemed they could not last,
        Small things and vast.

VII

There were those songs, a score times sung,
    With all their tripping tunes,
There were the laughters once that rung,
    There those unmatched full moons,
        Those idle noons!

VIII

There fadeless, fixed, were dust-dead flowers
    Remaining still in blow;
Elsewhere, wild love-makings in bowers;
    Hard by, that irised bow
        Of years ago.

IX

There were my ever memorable
    Glad days of pilgrimage,
Coiled like a precious parchment fell,
    Illumined page by page, -
        Unhurt by age.

X

' – Here you see spread those mortal ails
    So powerless to restrain
Your young life's eager hot assails,
    With hazards then not plain
        Till past their pain.

XI

'Here you see her who, by these laws
    You learn of, still shines on,
As pleasing-pure as erst she was,
    Though you think she lies yon,
        Graved, glow all gone.

XII

'Here are those others you used to prize. –
    But why go further we?
The Future? – Well, I would advise
    You let the future be,
        Unshown by me!

XIII

' 'Twould harrow you to see undraped
     The scenes in ripe array
That wait your globe – all worked and shaped;
     And I'll not, as I say,
          Bare them to-day.

XIV

'In fine, Time is a mock, – yea, such! –
     As he might well confess:
Yet hath he been believed in much,
     Though lately, under stress
          Of science, less.

XV

'And hence, of her you asked about
     At your first speaking: she
Hath, I assure you, not passed out
     Of continuity,
          But is in me.

XVI

'So thus doth Being's length transcend
     Time's ancient regal claim
To see all lengths begin and end.
     ''The Fourth Dimension'' fame
          Bruits as its name.'

New Year's Eve, 1922

'Let Me Enjoy'

I

LET me enjoy the earth no less
Because the all-enacting Might
That fashioned forth its loveliness
Had other aims than my delight.

II

About my path there flits a Fair,
Who throws me not a word or sign;
I'll charm me with her ignoring air,
And laud the lips not meant for mine.

III

From manuscripts of moving song
Inspired by scenes and dreams unknown
I'll pour out raptures that belong
To others, as they were my own.

IV

And some day hence, towards Paradise
And all its blest – if such should be –
I will lift glad, afar-off eyes,
Though it contain no place for me.

He Resolves to Say No More

O MY soul, keep the rest unknown!
It is too like a sound of moan
          When the charnel-eyed
          Pale Horse has nighed:
Yea, none shall gather what I hide!

Why load men's minds with more to bear
That bear already ails to spare?
          From now alway
          Till my last day
What I discern I will not say.

Let Time roll backward if it will;
(Magians who drive the midnight quill
          With brain aglow
          Can see it so,)
What I have learnt no man shall know.

And if my vision range beyond
The blinkered sight of souls in bond,
    – By truth made free –
    I'll let all be,
And show to no man what I see.

Going and Staying

I

THE moving sun-shapes on the spray,
The sparkles where the brook was flowing,
Pink faces, plightings, moonlit May,
These were the things we wished would stay;
    But they were going.

II

Seasons of blankness as of snow,
The silent bleed of a world decaying,
The moan of multitudes in woe,
These were the things we wished would go;
    But they were staying.

III

Then we looked closelier at Time,
And saw his ghostly arms revolving
To sweep off woeful things with prime,
Things sinister with things sublime
    Alike dissolving.

He Never Expected Much

[or]

A Consideration

[*A reflection*] *on My Eighty-Sixth Birthday*

WELL, World, you have kept faith with me,
        Kept faith with me;
Upon the whole you have proved to be
        Much as you said you were.
Since as a child I used to lie
Upon the leaze and watch the sky,
Never, I own, expected I
        That life would all be fair.

'Twas then you said, and since have said,
        Times since have said,
In that mysterious voice you shed
        From clouds and hills around:
'Many have loved me desperately,
Many with smooth serenity,
While some have shown contempt of me
        Till they dropped underground.

'I do not promise overmuch,
        Child; overmuch;
Just neutral-tinted haps and such,'
        You said to minds like mine.
Wise warning for your credit's sake!
Which I for one failed not to take,
And hence could stem such strain and ache
        As each year might assign.

II Nature's Look and Evidences

Nature's Questioning

WHEN I look forth at dawning, pool,
  Field, flock, and lonely tree,
  All seem to gaze at me
Like chastened children sitting silent in a school;

Their faces dulled, constrained, and worn,
  As though the master's ways
  Through the long teaching days
Had cowed them till their early zest was overborne.

Upon them stirs in lippings mere
  (As if once clear in call,
  But now scarce breathed at all) –
'We wonder, ever wonder, why we find us here!

'Has some Vast Imbecility,
  Mighty to build and blend,
  But impotent to tend,
Framed us in jest, and left us now to hazardry?

'Or come we of an Automaton
  Unconscious of our pains? . . .
  Or are we live remains
Of Godhead dying downwards, brain and eye now gone?

'Or is it that some high Plan betides,
  As yet not understood,
  Of Evil stormed by Good,
We the Forlorn Hope over which Achievement strides?'

Thus things around. No answerer I. . . .
  Meanwhile the winds, and rains,
  And Earth's old glooms and pains
Are still the same, and Life and Death are neighbours nigh.

Domicilium

It faces west, and round the back and sides
High beeches, bending, hang a veil of boughs,
And sweep against the roof. Wild honeysucks
Climb on the walls, and seem to sprout a wish
(If we may fancy wish of trees and plants)
To overtop the apple-trees hard by.

Red roses, lilacs, variegated box
Are there in plenty, and such hardy flowers
As flourish best untrained. Adjoining these
Are herbs and esculents; and farther still
A field; then cottages with trees, and last
The distant hills and sky.

Behind, the scene is wilder. Heath and furze
Are everything that seems to grow and thrive
Upon the uneven ground. A stunted thorn
Stands here and there, indeed; and from a pit
An oak uprises, springing from a seed
Dropped by some bird a hundred years ago.

                              In days bygone –
Long gone – my father's mother, who is now
Blest with the blest, would take me out to walk.
At such a time I once inquired of her
How looked the spot when first she settled here.
The answer I remember. 'Fifty years
Have passed since then, my child, and change has marked
The face of all things. Yonder garden-plots
And orchards were uncultivated slopes
O'ergrown with bramble bushes, furze and thorn:
That road a narrow path shut in by ferns,
Which, almost trees, obscured the passer-by.

'Our house stood quite alone, and those tall firs
And beeches were not planted. Snakes and efts
Swarmed in the summer days, and nightly bats
Would fly about our bedrooms. Heathcroppers
Lived on the hills, and were our only friends;
So wild it was when first we settled here.'

A Bird-Scene at a Rural Dwelling

WHEN the inmate stirs, the birds retire discreetly
From the window-ledge, whereon they whistled sweetly
     And on the step of the door,
     In the misty morning hoar;
   But now the dweller is up they flee
   To the crooked neighbouring codlin-tree;
And when he comes fully forth they seek the garden,
And call from the lofty costard, as pleading pardon
     For shouting so near before
     In their joy at being alive: –
Meanwhile the hammering clock within goes five.

I know a domicile of brown and green,
Where for a hundred summers there have been
Just such enactments, just such daybreaks seen.

At Middle-Field Gate in February

THE bars are thick with drops that show
     As they gather themselves from the fog
Like silver buttons ranged in a row,
And as evenly spaced as if measured, although
     They fall at the feeblest jog.

They load the leafless hedge hard by,
     And the blades of last year's grass,
While the fallow ploughland turned up nigh
In raw rolls, clammy and clogging lie –
     Too clogging for feet to pass.

How dry it was on a far-back day
     When straws hung the hedge and around,
When amid the sheaves in amorous play
In curtained bonnets and light array
     Bloomed a bevy now underground!

Bockhampton Lane

A Backward Spring

THE trees are afraid to put forth buds,
And there is timidity in the grass;
The plots lie gray where gouged by spuds,
 And whether next week will pass
Free of sly sour winds is the fret of each bush
 Of barberry waiting to bloom.

Yet the snowdrop's face betrays no gloom,
And the primrose pants in its heedless push,
Though the myrtle asks if it's worth the fight
 This year with frost and rime
 To venture one more time
On delicate leaves and buttons of white
From the selfsame bough as at last year's prime,
And never to ruminate on or remember
What happened to it in mid-December.

April 1917

An Unkindly May

A SHEPHERD stands by a gate in a white smock-frock:
He holds the gate ajar, intently counting his flock.

The sour spring wind is blurting boisterous-wise,
And bears on it dirty clouds across the skies;
Plantation timbers creak like rusty cranes,
And pigeons and rooks, dishevelled by late rains,
Are like gaunt vultures, sodden and unkempt,
And song-birds do not end what they attempt:
The buds have tried to open, but quite failing
Have pinched themselves together in their quailing.
The sun frowns whitely in eye-trying flaps
Through passing cloud-holes, mimicking audible taps.
'Nature, you're not commendable to-day!'
I think. 'Better to-morrow!' she seems to say.

That shepherd still stands in that white smock-frock,
Unnoting all things save the counting his flock.

Proud Songsters

THE thrushes sing as the sun is going,
And the finches whistle in ones and pairs,
And as it gets dark loud nightingales
      In bushes
Pipe, as they can when April wears,
   As if all Time were theirs.

These are brand-new birds of twelve-months' growing,
Which a year ago, or less than twain,
No finches were, nor nightingales,
      Nor thrushes,
But only particles of grain,
   And earth, and air, and rain.

At Day-Close in November

THE ten hours' light is abating,
   And a late bird wings across,
Where the pines, like waltzers waiting,
   Give their black heads a toss.

Beech leaves, that yellow the noon-time,
   Float past like specks in the eye;
I set every tree in my June time,
   And now they obscure the sky.

And the children who ramble through here
   Conceive that there never has been
A time when no tall trees grew here,
   That none will in time be seen.

Four in the Morning

AT four this day of June I rise:
The dawn-light strengthens steadily;
Earth is a cerule mystery,
As if not far from Paradise
            At four o'clock,

Or else near the Great Nebula,
Or where the Pleiads blink and smile:
(For though we see with eyes of guile
The grisly grin of things by day,
            At four o'clock

They show their best.) . . . In this vale's space
I am up the first, I think. Yet, no,
A whistling? and the to-and-fro
Wheezed whettings of a scythe apace
            At four o'clock? . . .

– Though pleasure spurred, I rose with irk:
Here is one at compulsion's whip
Taking his life's stern stewardship
With blithe uncare, and hard at work
            At four o'clock!

Bockhampton

The Sheep-Boy

A YAWNING, sunned concave
    Of purple, spread as an ocean wave
Entroughed on a morning of swell and sway
After a night when wind-fiends have been heard to rave:
Thus was the Heath called 'Draäts', on an August day.

Suddenly there intunes a hum:
This side, that side, it seems to come.

From the purple in myriads rise the bees
With consternation mid their rapt employ.
So headstrongly each speeds him past, and flees,
    As to strike the face of the shepherd-boy.
Awhile he waits, and wonders what they mean;
Till none is left upon the shagged demesne.

To learn what ails, the sheep-boy looks around;
    Behind him, out of the sea in swirls
    Flexuous and solid, clammy vapour-curls
Are rolling over Pokeswell Hills to the inland ground.
    Into the heath they sail,
    And travel up the vale
Like the moving pillar of cloud raised by the Israelite: –
In a trice the lonely sheep-boy seen so late ago,
        Draäts'-Hollow in gorgeous blow,
        And Kite-Hill's regal glow,
Are viewless – folded into those creeping scrolls of
    white.

On Rainbarrows

An August Midnight

I

A SHADED lamp and a waving blind,
And the beat of a clock from a distant floor:
On this scene enter – winged, horned, and spined –
A longlegs, a moth, and a dumbledore;
While 'mid my page there idly stands
A sleepy fly, that rubs its hands. . . .

II

Thus meet we five, in this still place,
At this point of time, at this point in space.
– My guests besmear my new-penned line,
Or bang at the lamp and fall supine.
'God's humblest, they!' I muse. Yet why?
They know Earth-secrets that know not I.

Max Gate, 1899

A Wet August

NINE drops of water bead the jessamine,
And nine-and-ninety smear the stones and tiles:
– 'Twas not so in that August – full-rayed, fine –
When we lived out-of-doors, sang songs, strode miles.

Or was there then no noted radiancy
Of summer? Were dun clouds, a dribbling bough,
Gilt over by the light I bore in me,
And was the waste world just the same as now?

It can have been so: yea, that threatenings
Of coming down-drip on the sunless gray,
By the then golden chances seen in things
Were wrought more bright than brightest skies to-day.

1920

Weathers

I

THIS is the weather the cuckoo likes,
        And so do I;
When showers betumble the chestnut spikes,
        And nestlings fly:
And the little brown nightingale bills his best,
And they sit outside at 'The Travellers' Rest',
And maids come forth sprig-muslin drest,
And citizens dream of the south and west,
        And so do I.

II

This is the weather the shepherd shuns,
        And so do I;
When beeches drip in browns and duns,
        And thresh, and ply;
And hill-hid tides throb, throe on throe,

And meadow rivulets overflow,
And drops on gate-bars hang in a row,
And rooks in families homeward go,
        And so do I.

Shortening Days at the Homestead

THE first fire since the summer is lit, and is smoking into the
        room:
    The sun-rays thread it through, like woof-lines in a loom.
    Sparrows spurt from the hedge, whom misgivings appal
That winter did not leave last year for ever, after all.
    Like shock-headed urchins, spiny-haired,
    Stand pollard willows, their twigs just bared.

Who is this coming with pondering pace,
Black and ruddy, with white embossed,
His eyes being black, and ruddy his face,
And the marge of his hair like morning frost?
        It's the cider-maker,
        And appletree-shaker,
And behind him on wheels, in readiness,
His mill, and tubs, and vat, and press.

Night-Time in Mid-Fall

IT is a storm-strid night, winds footing swift
        Through the blind profound;
    I know the happenings from their sound;
Leaves totter down still green, and spin and drift;
The tree-trunks rock to their roots, which wrench and lift
The loam where they run onward underground.

The streams are muddy and swollen; eels migrate
    To a new abode;
  Even cross, 'tis said, the turnpike-road;
(Men's feet have felt their crawl, home-coming late):
The westward fronts of towers are saturate,
Church-timbers crack, and witches ride abroad.

The Last Chrysanthemum

WHY should this flower delay so long
    To show its tremulous plumes?
Now is the time of plaintive robin-song,
    When flowers are in their tombs.

Through the slow summer, when the sun
    Called to each frond and whorl
That all he could for flowers was being done,
    Why did it not uncurl?

It must have felt that fervid call
    Although it took no heed,
Waking but now, when leaves like corpses fall,
    And saps all retrocede.

Too late its beauty, lonely thing,
    The season's shine is spent,
Nothing remains for it but shivering
    In tempests turbulent.

Had it a reason for delay,
    Dreaming in witlessness
That for a bloom so delicately gay
    Winter would stay its stress?

– I talk as if the thing were born
    With sense to work its mind;
Yet it is but one mask of many worn
    By the Great Face behind.

Lying Awake

You, Morningtide Star, now are steady-eyed, over the east,
    I know it as if I saw you;
You, Beeches, engrave on the sky your thin twigs, even the
        least;
    Had I paper and pencil I'd draw you.

You, Meadow, are white with your counterpane cover of
        dew,
    I see it as if I were there;
You, Churchyard, are lightening faint from the shade of the
        yew,
    The names creeping out everywhere.

'I Watched a Blackbird'

I watched a blackbird on a budding sycamore
One Easter Day, when sap was stirring twigs to the core;
    I saw his tongue, and crocus-coloured bill
    Parting and closing as he turned his trill;
    Then he flew down, seized on a stem of hay,
And upped to where his building scheme was under way,
As if so sure a nest were never shaped on spray.

We Field-Women

How it rained
When we worked at Flintcomb-Ash,
And could not stand upon the hill
Trimming swedes for the slicing-mill.
The wet washed through us – plash, plash, plash:
How it rained!

How it snowed
When we crossed from Flintcomb-Ash
To the Great Barn for drawing reed,
Since we could nowise chop a swede. –
Flakes in each doorway and casement-sash:
How it snowed!

How it shone
When we went from Flintcomb-Ash
To start at dairywork once more
In the laughing meads, with cows three-score,
And pails, and songs, and love – too rash:
How it shone!

Snow in the Suburbs

EVERY branch big with it,
Bent every twig with it;
Every fork like a white web-foot;
Every street and pavement mute:
Some flakes have lost their way, and grope back upward,
when
Meeting those meandering down they turn and descend
again.
The palings are glued together like a wall,
And there is no waft of wind with the fleecy fall.

A sparrow enters the tree,
Whereon immediately
A snow-lump thrice his own slight size
Descends on him and showers his head and eyes,
And overturns him,
And near inurns him,
And lights on a nether twig, when its brush
Starts off a volley of other lodging lumps with a rush.

The steps are a blanched slope,
Up which, with feeble hope,
A black cat comes, wide-eyed and thin;
And we take him in.

A Light Snow-Fall after Frost

ON the flat road a man at last appears:
    How much his whitening hairs
Owe to the settling snow's mute anchorage,
And how much to a life's rough pilgrimage,
    One cannot certify.

    The frost is on the wane,
The cobwebs hanging close outside the pane
Pose as festoons of thick white worsted there,
Of their pale presence no eye being aware
    Till the rime made them plain.

    A second man comes by;
His ruddy beard brings fire to the pallid scene:
    His coat is faded green;
    Hence seems it that his mien
    Wears something of the dye
Of the berried holm-trees that he passes nigh.

The snow-feathers so gently swoop that though
    But half an hour ago
The road was brown, and now is starkly white,
A watcher would have failed defining quite
    When it transformed it so.

Near Surbiton

The Fallow Deer at the Lonely House

ONE without looks in to-night
    Through the curtain-chink
From the sheet of glistening white;
One without looks in to-night
    As we sit and think
    By the fender-brink.

We do not discern those eyes
    Watching in the snow;
Lit by lamps of rosy dyes
We do not discern those eyes
    Wondering, aglow,
    Fourfooted, tiptoe.

The Year's Awakening

How do you know that the pilgrim track
Along the belting zodiac
Swept by the sun in his seeming rounds
Is traced by now to the Fishes' bounds
And into the Ram, when weeks of cloud
Have wrapt the sky in a clammy shroud,
And never as yet a tint of spring
Has shown in the Earth's apparelling;
    O vespering bird, how do you know,
      How do you know?

How do you know, deep underground,
Hid in your bed from sight and sound,
Without a turn in temperature,
With weather life can scarce endure,
That light has won a fraction's strength,
And day put on some moments' length,
Whereof in merest rote will come,
Weeks hence, mild airs that do not numb;
    O crocus root, how do you know,
      How do you know?

February 1910

At a Lunar Eclipse

THY shadow, Earth, from Pole to Central Sea,
Now steals along upon the Moon's meek shine
In even monochrome and curving line
Of imperturbable serenity.

How shall I link such sun-cast symmetry
With the torn troubled form I know as thine,
That profile, placid as a brow divine,
With continents of moil and misery?

And can immense Mortality but throw
So small a shade, and Heaven's high human scheme
Be hemmed within the coasts yon arc implies?

Is such the stellar gauge of earthly show,
Nation at war with nation, brains that teem,
Heroes, and women fairer than the skies?

Once at Swanage

THE spray sprang up across the cusps of the moon,
  And all its light loomed green
  As a witch-flame's weirdsome sheen
At the minute of an incantation scene;
And it greened our gaze – that night at demilune.

Roaring high and roaring low was the sea
  Behind the headland shores:
  It symboled the slamming of doors,
Or a regiment hurrying over hollow floors. . . .
And there we two stood, hands clasped; I and she!

Shut Out That Moon

CLOSE up the casement, draw the blind,
    Shut out that stealing moon,
She wears too much the guise she wore
    Before our lutes were strewn
With years-deep dust, and names we read
    On a white stone were hewn.

Step not forth on the dew-dashed lawn
    To view the Lady's Chair,
Immense Orion's glittering form,
    The Less and Greater Bear:
Stay in; to such sights we were drawn
    When faded ones were fair.

Brush not the bough for midnight scents
    That come forth lingeringly,
And wake the same sweet sentiments
    They breathed to you and me
When living seemed a laugh, and love
    All it was said to be.

Within the common lamp-lit room
    Prison my eyes and thought;
Let dingy details crudely loom,
    Mechanic speech be wrought:
Too fragrant was Life's early bloom,
    Too tart the fruit it brought!

1904

The Darkling Thrush

I LEANT upon a coppice gate
    When Frost was spectre-gray,
And Winter's dregs made desolate
    The weakening eye of day.
The tangled bine-stems scored the sky
    Like strings of broken lyres,
And all mankind that haunted nigh
    Had sought their household fires.

The land's sharp features seemed to be
    The Century's corpse outleant,
His crypt the cloudy canopy,
    The wind his death-lament.
The ancient pulse of germ and birth
    Was shrunken hard and dry,
And every spirit upon earth
    Seemed fervourless as I.

At once a voice arose among
    The bleak twigs overhead
In a full-hearted evensong
    Of joy illimited;
An aged thrush, frail, gaunt, and small,
    In blast-beruffled plume,
Had chosen thus to fling his soul
    Upon the growing gloom.

So little cause for carolings
    Of such ecstatic sound
Was written on terrestrial things
    Afar or nigh around,
That I could think there trembled through
    His happy good-night air
Some blessed Hope, whereof he knew
    And I was unaware.

31 December 1900

Birds at Winter Nightfall

(Triolet)

AROUND the house the flakes fly faster,
And all the berries now are gone
From holly and cotonea-aster
Around the house. The flakes fly! – faster
Shutting indoors that crumb-outcaster
We used to see upon the lawn
Around the house. The flakes fly faster,
And all the berries now are gone!

Max Gate

Afterwards

WHEN the Present has latched its postern behind my
    tremulous stay,
  And the May month flaps its glad green leaves like wings,
Delicate-filmed as new-spun silk, will the neighbours say,
  'He was a man who used to notice such things'?

If it be in the dusk when, like an eyelid's soundless blink,
  The dewfall-hawk comes crossing the shades to alight
Upon the wind-warped upland thorn, a gazer may think,
  'To him this must have been a familiar sight.'

If I pass during some nocturnal blackness, mothy and warm,
  When the hedgehog travels furtively over the lawn,
One may say, 'He strove that such innocent creatures should
    come to no harm,
  But he could do little for them; and now he is gone.'

If, when hearing that I have been stilled at last, they stand at
    the door,
  Watching the full-starred heavens that winter sees,
Will this thought rise on those who will meet my face no
    more,
  'He was one who had an eye for such mysteries'?

And will any say when my bell of quittance is heard in the
    gloom,
  And a crossing breeze cuts a pause in its outrollings,
Till they rise again, as they were a new bell's boom,
  'He hears it not now, but used to notice such things'?

III Men, Women, Places

At the Aquatic Sports

WITH their backs to the sea two fiddlers stand
Facing the concourse on the strand,
    And a third man who sings.
The sports proceed; there are crab-catchings;
The people laugh as levity spreads;
Yet these three do not turn their heads
    To see whence the merriment springs.

They cease their music, but even then
They stand as before, do those three men,
    Though pausing, nought to do:
They never face to the seaward view
To enjoy the contests, add their cheer,
So wholly is their being here
    A business they pursue.

Satires of Circumstance

I. At Tea

THE kettle descants in a cosy drone,
And the young wife looks in her husband's face,
And then at her guest's, and shows in her own
Her sense that she fills an envied place;
And the visiting lady is all abloom,
And says there was never so sweet a room.

And the happy young housewife does not know
That the woman beside her was first his choice,
Till the fates ordained it could not be so. . . .
Betraying nothing in look or voice
The guest sits smiling and sips her tea,
And he throws her a stray glance yearningly.

II. *In Church*

'AND now to God the Father,' he ends,
And his voice thrills up to the topmost tiles:
Each listener chokes as he bows and bends,
And emotion pervades the crowded aisles.
Then the preacher glides to the vestry-door,
And shuts it, and thinks he is seen no more.

The door swings softly ajar meanwhile,
And a pupil of his in the Bible class,
Who adores him as one without gloss or guile,
Sees her idol stand with a satisfied smile
And re-enact at the vestry-glass
Each pulpit gesture in deft dumb-show
That had moved the congregation so.

VI. *In the Cemetery*

'YOU see those mothers squabbling there?'
Remarks the man of the cemetery.
'One says in tears, "'Tis mine lies here!"
Another, "Nay, mine, you Pharisee!"
Another, "How dare you move my flowers
And put your own on this grave of ours!"
But all their children were laid therein
At different times, like sprats in a tin.

'And then the main drain had to cross,
And we moved the lot some nights ago,
And packed them away in the general foss
With hundreds more. But their folks don't know,
And as well cry over a new-laid drain
As anything else, to ease your pain!'

VII. *Outside the Window*

'MY stick!' he says, and turns in the lane
To the house just left, whence a vixen voice
Comes out with the firelight through the pane,
And he sees within that the girl of his choice
Stands rating her mother with eyes aglare
For something said while he was there.

'At last I behold her soul undraped!'
Thinks the man who had loved her more than himself;
'My God! – 'tis but narrowly I have escaped. –
My precious porcelain proves it delf.'
His face has reddened like one ashamed,
And he steals off, leaving his stick unclaimed.

VIII. *In the Study*

HE enters, and mute on the edge of a chair
Sits a thin-faced lady, a stranger there,
A type of decayed gentility;
And by some small signs he well can guess
That she comes to him almost breakfastless.

'I have called – I hope I do not err –
I am looking for a purchaser
Of some score volumes of the works
Of eminent divines I own, –
Left by my father – though it irks

My patience to offer them.' And she smiles
As if necessity were unknown;
'But the truth of it is that oftenwhiles
I have wished, as I am fond of art,
To make my rooms a little smart,
And these old books are so in the way.'

And lightly still she laughs to him,
As if to sell were a mere gay whim,
And that, to be frank, Life were indeed
To her not vinegar and gall,
But fresh and honey-like; and Need
No household skeleton at all.

XII. At the Draper's

'I STOOD at the back of the shop, my dear,
      But you did not perceive me.
Well, when they deliver what you were shown
      I shall know nothing of it, believe me!'

And he coughed and coughed as she paled and said,
      'O, I didn't see you come in there –
Why couldn't you speak?' – 'Well, I didn't. I left
      That you should not notice I'd been there.

'You were viewing some lovely things. "*Soon required
      For a widow, of latest fashion;*"
And I knew 'twould upset you to meet the man
      Who had to be cold and ashen

'And screwed in a box before they could dress you
      "*In the last new note in mourning,*"
As they defined it. So, not to distress you,
      I left you to your adorning.'

XV. *In the Moonlight*

'O LONELY workman, standing there
In a dream, why do you stare and stare
At her grave, as no other grave there were?

'If your great gaunt eyes so importune
Her soul by the shine of this corpse-cold moon
Maybe you'll raise her phantom soon!'

'Why, fool, it is what I would rather see
Than all the living folk there be;
But alas, there is no such joy for me!'

'Ah – she was one you loved, no doubt,
Through good and evil, through rain and drought,
And when she passed, all your sun went out?'

'Nay: she was the woman I did not love,
Whom all the others were ranked above,
Whom during her life I thought nothing of.'

A Sheep Fair

THE day arrives of the autumn fair,
       And torrents fall,
Though sheep in throngs are gathered there,
       Ten thousand all,
Sodden, with hurdles round them reared:
And, lot by lot, the pens are cleared,
And the auctioneer wrings out his beard,
And wipes his book, bedrenched and smeared,
And rakes the rain from his face with the edge of his hand,
       As torrents fall.

The wool of the ewes is like a sponge
       With the daylong rain:
Jammed tight, to turn, or lie, or lunge,
       They strive in vain.

Their horns are soft as finger-nails,
Their shepherds reek against the rails,
The tied dogs soak with tucked-in tails,
The buyers' hat-brims fill like pails,
Which spill small cascades when they shift their stand
       In the daylong rain.

POSTSCRIPT

Time has trailed lengthily since met
      At Pummery Fair
Those panting thousands in their wet
      And woolly wear:
And every flock long since has bled,
And all the dripping buyers have sped,
And the hoarse auctioneer is dead,
Who 'Going – going!' so often said,
As he consigned to doom each meek, mewed band
      At Pummery Fair.

Last Look round St Martin's Fair

THE sun is like an open furnace door,
Whose round revealed retort confines the roar
      Of fires beyond terrene;
The moon presents the lustre-lacking face
      Of a brass dial gone green,
      Whose hours no eye can trace.
The unsold heathcroppers are driven home
To the shades of the Great Forest whence they come
By men with long cord-waistcoats in brown monochrome.
      The stars break out, and flicker in the breeze,
      It seems, that twitches the trees. –
      From its hot idol soon
The fickle unresting earth has turned to a fresh patroon –
      The cold, now brighter, moon.
      The woman in red, at the nut-stall with the gun,
      Lights up, and still goes on:
She's redder in the flare-lamp than the sun
      Showed it ere it was gone.

Her hands are black with loading all the day,
And yet she treats her labour as 'twere play,
Tosses her ear-rings, and talks ribaldry
To the young men around as natural gaiety,
  And not a weary work she'd readily stay,
    And never again nut-shooting see,
    Though crying, 'Fire away!'

Expectation and Experience

'I HAD a holiday once,' said the woman –
  Her name I did not know –
'And I thought that where I'd like to go,
Of all the places for being jolly,
And getting rid of melancholy,
  Would be to a good big fair:
And I went. And it rained in torrents, drenching
Every horse, and sheep, and yeoman,
  And my shoulders, face and hair;
And I found that I was the single woman
  In the field – and looked quite odd there!
Everything was spirit-quenching:
I crept and stood in the lew of a wall
To think, and could not tell at all
  What on earth made me plod there!'

Coming Up Oxford Street: Evening

THE sun from the west glares back,
And the sun from the watered track,
And the sun from the sheets of glass,
And the sun from each window-brass;
Sun-mirrorings, too, brighten
From show-cases beneath
The laughing eyes and teeth
Of ladies who rouge and whiten.

And the same warm god explores
Panels and chinks of doors;
Problems with chymists' bottles
Profound as Aristotle's
He solves, and with good cause,
Having been ere man was.

Also he dazzles the pupils of one who walks west,
A city-clerk, with eyesight not of the best,
Who sees no escape to the very verge of his days
From the rut of Oxford Street into open ways;
And he goes along with head and eyes flagging forlorn,
Empty of interest in things, and wondering why he was
  born.

As seen 4 July 1872

'She Charged Me'

SHE charged me with having said this and that
To another woman long years before,
In the very parlour where we sat, –

Sat on a night when the endless pour
Of rain on the roof and the road below
Bent the spring of the spirit more and more. . . .

– So charged she me; and the Cupid's bow
Of her mouth was hard, and her eyes, and her face,
And her white forefinger lifted slow.

Had she done it gently, or shown a trace
That not too curiously would she view
A folly flown ere her reign had place,

A kiss might have closed it. But I knew
From the fall of each word, and the pause between,
That the curtain would drop upon us two
Ere long, in our play of slave and queen.

The Newcomer's Wife

HE paused on the sill of a door ajar
That screened a lively liquor-bar,
For the name had reached him through the door
Of her he had married the week before.

'We called her the Hack of the Parade;
But she was discreet in the games she played;
If slightly worn, she's pretty yet,
And gossips, after all, forget:

'And he knows nothing of her past;
I am glad the girl's in luck at last;
Such ones, though stale to native eyes,
Newcomers snatch at as a prize.'

'Yes, being a stranger he sees her blent
Of all that's fresh and innocent,
Nor dreams how many a love-campaign
She had enjoyed before his reign!'

That night there was the splash of a fall
Over the slimy harbour-wall:
They searched, and at the deepest place
Found him with crabs upon his face.

Cynic's Epitaph

A RACE with the sun as he downed
         I ran at evetide,
Intent who should first gain the ground
         And there hide.

He beat me by some minutes then,
         But I triumphed anon,
For when he'd to rise up again
         I stayed on.

Epitaph on a Pessimist

I'M Smith of Stoke, aged sixty-odd,
    I've lived without a dame
From youth-time on; and would to God
    My dad had done the same.

From the French and Greek

The Bird-Catcher's Boy

'FATHER, I fear your trade:
    Surely it's wrong!
Little birds limed and made
    Captive life-long.

'Larks bruise and bleed in jail,
    Trying to rise;
Every caged nightingale
    Soon pines and dies.'

'Don't be a dolt, my boy!
    Birds must be caught;
My lot is such employ,
    Yours to be taught.

'Soft shallow stuff as that
    Out from your head!
Just learn your lessons pat,
    Then off to bed.'

Lightless, without a word
    Bedwise he fares;
Groping his way is heard
    Seek the dark stairs

Through the long passage, where
    Hang the caged choirs:
Harp-like his fingers there
    Sweep on the wires.

Next day, at dye of dawn,
　Freddy was missed:
Whither the boy had gone
　Nobody wist.

That week, the next one, whiled:
　No news of him:
Weeks up to months were piled:
　Hope dwindled dim.

Yet not a single night
　Locked they the door,
Waiting, heart-sick, to sight
　Freddy once more.

Hopping there long anon
　Still the birds hung:
Like those in Babylon
　Captive, they sung.

One wintry Christmastide
　Both lay awake;
All cheer within them dried,
　Each hour an ache.

Then some one seemed to flit
　Soft in below;
'Freddy's come!' Up they sit,
　Faces aglow.

Thereat a groping touch
　Dragged on the wires
Lightly and softly – much
　As they were lyres;

'Just as it used to be
　When he came in,
Feeling in darkness the
　Stairway to win!'

Waiting a trice or two
　Yet, in the gloom,
Both parents pressed into
　Freddy's old room.

There on the empty bed
    White the moon shone,
As ever since they'd said,
    'Freddy is gone!'

That night at Durdle-Door[1]
    Foundered a hoy,
And the tide washed ashore
    One sailor boy.

21 November 1912

Midnight on the Great Western

IN the third-class seat sat the journeying boy,
    And the roof-lamp's oily flame
Played down on his listless form and face,
Bewrapt past knowing to what he was going,
    Or whence he came.

In the band of his hat the journeying boy
    Had a ticket stuck; and a string
Around his neck bore the key of his box,
That twinkled gleams of the lamp's sad beams
    Like a living thing.

What past can be yours, O journeying boy
    Towards a world unknown,
Who calmly, as if incurious quite
On all at stake, can undertake
    This plunge alone?

Knows your soul a sphere, O journeying boy,
    Our rude realms far above,
Whence with spacious vision you mark and mete
This region of sin that you find you in,
    But are not of?

[1] Durdle-Door, a rock on the South coast

The New Toy

SHE cannot leave it alone,
    The new toy;
She pats it, smooths it, rights it, to show it's her own,
As the other train-passengers muse on its temper and tone,
    Till she draws from it cries of annoy: –
She feigns to appear as if thinking it nothing so rare
    Or worthy of pride, to achieve
This wonder a child, though with reason the rest of them
    there
    May so be inclined to believe.

At the Railway Station, Upway

'THERE is not much that I can do,
    For I've no money that's quite my own!'
    Spoke up the pitying child –
A little boy with a violin
At the station before the train came in, –
'But I can play my fiddle to you,
And a nice one 'tis, and good in tone!'

    The man in the handcuffs smiled;
The constable looked, and he smiled, too,
    As the fiddle began to twang;
And the man in the handcuffs suddenly sang
        With grimful glee:
        'This life so free
        Is the thing for me!'
And the constable smiled, and said no word,
As if unconscious of what he heard;
And so they went on till the train came in –
The convict, and boy with the violin.

The Whitewashed Wall

WHY does she turn in that shy soft way
    Whenever she stirs the fire,
And kiss to the chimney-corner wall,
    As if entranced to admire
Its whitewashed bareness more than the sight
    Of a rose in richest green?
I have known her long, but this raptured rite
    I never before have seen.

– Well, once when her son cast his shadow there,
    A friend took a pencil and drew him
Upon that flame-lit wall. And the lines
    Had a lifelike semblance to him.
And there long stayed his familiar look;
    But one day, ere she knew,
The whitener came to cleanse the nook,
    And covered the face from view.

'Yes,' he said: 'My brush goes on with a rush,
    And the draught is buried under;
When you have to whiten old cots and brighten,
    What else can you do, I wonder?'
But she knows he's there. And when she yearns
    For him, deep in the labouring night,
She sees him as close at hand, and turns
    To him under his sheet of white.

One We Knew

(*M.H. 1772–1857*)

SHE told how they used to form for the country dances –
    'The Triumph', 'The New-rigged Ship' –
To the light of the guttering wax in the panelled manses,
    And in cots to the blink of a dip.

She spoke of the wild 'poussetting' and 'allemanding'
    On carpet, on oak, and on sod;
And the two long rows of ladies and gentlemen standing,
    And the figures the couples trod.

She showed us the spot where the maypole was yearly
       planted,
    And where the bandsmen stood
While breeched and kerchiefed partners whirled, and panted
    To choose each other for good.

She told of that far-back day when they learnt astounded
    Of the death of the King of France:
Of the Terror; and then of Bonaparte's unbounded
    Ambition and arrogance.

Of how his threats woke warlike preparations
    Along the southern strand,
And how each night brought tremors and trepidations
    Lest morning should see him land.

She said she had often heard the gibbet creaking
    As it swayed in the lightning flash,
Had caught from the neighbouring town a small child's
       shrieking
    At the cart-tail under the lash. . . .

With cap-framed face and long gaze into the embers –
    We seated around her knees –
She would dwell on such dead themes, not as one who
       remembers,
    But rather as one who sees.

She seemed one left behind of a band gone distant
    So far that no tongue could hail:
Past things retold were to her as things existent,
    Things present but as a tale.

20 May 1902

A Church Romance

(*Mellstock: circa 1835*)

SHE turned in the high pew, until her sight
Swept the west gallery, and caught its row
Of music-men with viol, book, and bow
Against the sinking sad tower-window light.

She turned again; and in her pride's despite
One strenuous viol's inspirer seemed to throw
A message from his string to her below,
Which said: 'I claim thee as my own forthright!'

Thus their hearts' bond began, in due time signed.
And long years thence, when Age had scared
      Romance,
At some old attitude of his or glance
That gallery-scene would break upon her mind,
With him as minstrel, ardent, young, and trim,
Bowing 'New Sabbath' or 'Mount Ephraim'.

After the Last Breath

(*J.H. 1813–1904*)

THERE'S no more to be done, or feared, or hoped;
None now need watch, speak low, and list, and tire;
No irksome crease outsmoothed, no pillow sloped
      Does she require.

Blankly we gaze. We are free to go or stay;
Our morrow's anxious plans have missed their aim;
Whether we leave to-night or wait till day
      Counts as the same.

The lettered vessels of medicaments
Seem asking wherefore we have set them here;

Each palliative its silly face presents
    As useless gear.

And yet we feel that something savours well;
We note a numb relief withheld before;
Our well-beloved is prisoner in the cell
    Of Time no more.

We see by littles now the deft achievement
Whereby she has escaped the Wrongers all,
In view of which our momentary bereavement
    Outshapes but small.

   1904

Logs on the Hearth

A Memory of a Sister

THE fire advances along the log
    Of the tree we felled,
Which bloomed and bore striped apples by the peck
    Till its last hour of bearing knelled.

The fork that first my hand would reach
    And then my foot
In climbings upward inch by inch, lies now
    Sawn, sapless, darkening with soot.

Where the bark chars is where, one year,
    It was pruned, and bled –
Then overgrew the wound. But now, at last,
    Its growings all have stagnated.

My fellow-climber rises dim
    From her chilly grave –
Just as she was, her foot near mine on the bending limb,
    Laughing, her young brown hand awave.

December 1915

Molly Gone

No more summer for Molly and me;
    There is snow on the tree,
And the blackbirds plump large as the rooks are, almost,
    And the water is hard
Where they used to dip bills at the dawn ere her figure was
        lost
    To these coasts, now my prison close-barred.

No more planting by Molly and me
    Where the beds used to be
Of sweet-william; no training the clambering rose
    By the framework of fir
Now bowering the pathway, whereon it swings gaily and
        blows
    As if calling commendment from her.

No more jauntings by Molly and me
    To the town by the sea,
Or along over Whitesheet to Wynyard's green Gap,
    Catching Montacute Crest
To the right against Sedgmoor, and Corton-Hill's far-distant
        cap,
    And Pilsdon and Lewsdon to west.

No more singing by Molly to me
    In the evenings when she
Was in mood and in voice, and the candles were lit,
    And past the porch-quoin
The rays would spring out on the laurels; and dumbledores
        hit
    On the pane, as if wishing to join.

Where, then, is Molly, who's no more with me?
    – As I stand on this lea,
Thinking thus, there's a many-flamed star in the air,
    That tosses a sign
That her glance is regarding its face from her home, so that
        there
    Her eyes may have meetings with mine.

Standing by the Mantelpiece

(*H.M.M.*, 1873)

THIS candle-wax is shaping to a shroud
To-night. (They call it that, as you may know) –
By touching it the claimant is avowed,
And hence I press it with my finger – so.

To-night. To me twice night, that should have been
The radiance of the midmost tick of noon,
And close around me wintertime is seen
That might have shone the veriest day of June!

But since all's lost, and nothing really lies
Above but shade, and shadier shade below,
Let me make clear, before one of us dies,
My mind to yours, just now embittered so.

Since you agreed, unurged and full-advised,
And let warmth grow without discouragement,
Why do you bear you now as if surprised,
When what has come was clearly consequent?

Since you have spoken, and finality
Closes around, and my last movements loom,
I say no more: the rest must wait till we
Are face to face again, yonside the tomb.

And let the candle-wax thus mould a shape
Whose meaning now, if hid before, you know,
And how by touch one present claims its drape,
And that it's I who press my finger – so.

Barthélémon at Vauxhall

François Hippolite Barthélémon, first-fiddler at Vauxhall Gardens, composed what was probably the most popular morning hymn-tune ever written. It was formerly sung, full-voiced, every Sunday in most churches, to Bishop Ken's words, but is now seldom heard.

HE said: 'Awake my soul, and with the sun,' . . .
And paused upon the bridge, his eyes due east,
Where was emerging like a full-robed priest
The irradiate globe that vouched the dark as done.

It lit his face – the weary face of one
Who in the adjacent gardens charged his string,
Nightly, with many a tuneful tender thing,
Till stars were weak, and dancing hours outrun.

And then were threads of matin music spun
In trial tones as he pursued his way:
'This is a morn,' he murmured, 'well begun:
This strain to Ken will count when I am clay!'

And count it did; till, caught by echoing lyres,
It spread to galleried naves and mighty quires.

The Last Signal

(11 Oct. 1886)

A Memory of William Barnes

SILENTLY I footed by an uphill road
    That led from my abode to a spot yew-boughed;
Yellowly the sun sloped low down to westward,
    And dark was the east with cloud.

Then, amid the shadow of that livid sad east,
    Where the light was least, and a gate stood wide,
Something flashed the fire of the sun that was facing it,
    Like a brief blaze on that side.

Looking hard and harder I knew what it meant –
The sudden shine sent from the livid east scene;
It meant the west mirrored by the coffin of my friend there,
    Turning to the road from his green,

To take his last journey forth – he who in his prime
  Trudged so many a time from that gate athwart the land!
Thus a farewell to me he signalled on his grave-way,
    As with a wave of his hand.

Winterborne-Came Path

The Schreckhorn

(*With thoughts of Leslie Stephen*)
(*June 1897*)

ALOOF, as if a thing of mood and whim;
Now that its spare and desolate figure gleams
Upon my nearing vision, less it seems
A looming Alp-height than a guise of him
Who scaled its horn with ventured life and limb,
Drawn on by vague imaginings, maybe,
Of semblance to his personality
In its quaint glooms, keen lights, and rugged trim.

At his last change, when Life's dull coils unwind,
Will he, in old love, hitherward escape,
And the eternal essence of his mind
Enter this silent adamantine shape,
And his low voicing haunt its slipping snows
When dawn that calls the climber dyes them rose?

A Watering-Place Lady Inventoried

A SWEETNESS of temper unsurpassed and unforgettable,
A mole on the cheek whose absence would have been
     regrettable,
A ripple of pleasant converse full of modulation,
A bearing of inconveniences without vexation,
Till a cynic would find her amiability provoking,
Tempting him to indulge in mean and wicked joking.

Flawlessly oval of face, especially cheek and chin,
With a glance of a quality that beckoned for a glance akin,
A habit of swift assent to any intelligence broken,
Before the fact to be conveyed was fully spoken
And she could know to what her colloquist would win her, –
This from a too alive impulsion to sympathy in her, –
All with a sense of the ridiculous, keen yet charitable;
In brief, a rich, profuse attractiveness unnarratable.

I should have added her hints that her husband prized her
     but slenderly,
And that (with a sigh) 'twas a pity she'd no one to treat her
     tenderly.

News for Her Mother

I

ONE mile more is
Where your door is,
     Mother mine! –
Harvest's coming,
Mills are strumming,
     Apples fine,
And the cider made to-year will be as wine.

II

Yet, not viewing
What's a-doing
    Here around
Is it thrills me,
And so fills me
    That I bound
Like a ball or leaf or lamb along the ground.

III

Tremble not now
At your lot now,
    Silly soul!
Hosts have sped them
Quick to wed them,
    Great and small,
Since the first two sighing half-hearts made a whole.

IV

Yet I wonder,
Will it sunder
    Her from me?
Will she guess that
I said 'Yes,' – that
    His I'd be,
Ere I thought she might not see him as I see!

V

Old brown gable,
Granary, stable,
    Here you are!
O my mother,
Can another
    Ever bar
Mine from thy heart, make thy nearness seem afar?

The Lady in the Furs

'I'M a lofty lovely woman,'
 Says the lady in the furs,
In the glance she throws around her
 On the poorer dames and sirs:
'This robe, that cost three figures,
 Yes, is mine,' her nod avers.

'True, my money did not buy it,
 But my husband's, from the trade;
And they, they only got it
 From things feeble and afraid
By murdering them in ambush
 With a cunning engine's aid.

'True, my hands, too, did not shape it
 To the pretty cut you see,
But the hands of midnight workers
 Who are strangers quite to me:
It was fitted, too, by dressers
 Ranged around me toilsomely.

'But I am a lovely lady,
 Though sneerers say I shine
By robbing Nature's children
 Of apparel not mine,
And that I am but a broom-stick,
 Like a scarecrow's wooden spine.'

  1925

The Ruined Maid

'O 'MELIA, my dear, this does everything crown!
Who could have supposed I should meet you in Town?
And whence such fair garments, such prosperi-ty?' –
'O didn't you know I'd been ruined?' said she.

– 'You left us in tatters, without shoes or socks,
Tired of digging potatoes, and spudding up docks;
And now you've gay bracelets and bright feathers three!' –
'Yes: that's how we dress when we're ruined,' said she.

– 'At home in the barton you said "thee" and "thou",
And "thik oon", and "theäs oon", and "t'other"; but now
Your talking quite fits 'ee for high compa-ny!' –
'Some polish is gained with one's ruin,' said she.

– 'Your hands were like paws then, your face blue and bleak
But now I'm bewitched by your delicate cheek,
And your little gloves fit as on any la-dy!' –
'We never do work when we're ruined,' said she.

– 'You used to call home-life a hag-ridden dream,
And you'd sigh, and you'd sock; but at present you seem
To know not of megrims or melancho-ly!' –
'True. One's pretty lively when ruined,' said she.

– 'I wish I had feathers, a fine sweeping gown,
And a delicate face, and could strut about Town!' –
'My dear – a raw country girl, such as you be,
Cannot quite expect that. You ain't ruined,' said she.

Westbourne Park Villas, 1866

That Kiss in the Dark

RECALL it you? –
Say you do! –
When you went out into the night,
In an impatience that would not wait,
From that lone house in the woodland spot,
And when I, thinking you had gone
For ever and ever from my sight,
Came after, printing a kiss upon
Black air
In my despair,
And my two lips lit on your cheek

As you leant silent against a gate,
Making my woman's face flush hot
At what I had done in the dark, unware
You lingered for me but would not speak:
Yes, kissed you, thinking you were not there!
                Recall it you? –
                Say you do!

The Young Glass-Stainer

'THESE Gothic windows, how they wear me out
With cusp and foil, and nothing straight or square,
Crude colours, leaden borders roundabout,
And fitting in Peter here, and Matthew there!

'What a vocation! Here do I draw now
The abnormal, loving the Hellenic norm;
Martha I paint, and dream of Hera's brow,
Mary, and think of Aphrodite's form.'

Nov. 1893

The Curate's Kindness

A Workhouse Irony

I

I THOUGHT they'd be strangers aroun' me,
        But she's to be there!
Let me jump out o' waggon and go back and drown me
        At Pummery or Ten-Hatches Weir.

II

I thought: 'Well, I've come to the Union –
        The workhouse at last –

After honest hard work all the week, and Communion
  O' Zundays, these fifty years past.

III

' 'Tis hard; but,' I thought, 'never mind it:
    There's gain in the end:
And when I get used to the place I shall find it
    A home, and may find there a friend.

IV

'Life there will be better than t'other,
    For peace is assured.
The men in one wing and their wives in another
    Is strictly the rule of the Board.'

V

Just then one young Pa'son arriving
    Steps up out of breath
To the side o' the waggon wherein we were driving
    To Union; and calls out and saith:

VI

'Old folks, that harsh order is altered,
    Be not sick of heart!
The Guardians they poohed and they pished and they
       paltered
    When urged not to keep you apart.

VII

' "It is wrong," I maintained, "to divide them,
    Near forty years wed."
"Very well, sir. We promise, then, they shall abide them
    In one wing together," they said.'

VIII

Then I sank – knew 'twas quite a foredone thing
    That misery should be
To the end! . . . To get freed of her there was the one thing
    Had made the change welcome to me.

IX

To go there was ending but badly;
   'Twas shame and 'twas pain;
'But anyhow,' thought I, 'thereby I shall gladly
   Get free of this forty years' chain.'

X

I thought they'd be strangers aroun' me,
   But she's to be there!
Let me jump out o' waggon and go back and drown me
   At Pummery or Ten-Hatches Weir.

In a Waiting-Room

ON a morning sick as the day of doom
   With the drizzling gray
   Of an English May,
There were few in the railway waiting-room.
About its walls were framed and varnished
Pictures of liners, fly-blown, tarnished.
The table bore a Testament
For travellers' reading, if suchwise bent.

   I read it on and on,
And, thronging the Gospel of Saint John,
Were figures – additions, multiplications –
By some one scrawled, with sundry emendations;
   Not scoffingly designed,
   But with an absent mind, –
Plainly a bagman's counts of cost,
What he had profited, what lost;
And whilst I wondered if there could have been
   Any particle of a soul
   In that poor man at all,
   To cypher rates of wage
   Upon that printed page,
   There joined in the charmless scene
And stood over me and the scribbled book

(To lend the hour's mean hue
A smear of tragedy too)
A soldier and wife, with haggard look
Subdued to stone by strong endeavour;
And then I heard
From a casual word
They were parting as they believed for ever.

But next there came
Like the eastern flame
Of some high altar, children – a pair –
Who laughed at the fly-blown pictures there.
'Here are the lovely ships that we,
Mother, are by and by going to see!
When we get there it's 'most sure to be fine,
And the band will play, and the sun will shine!'

It rained on the skylight with a din
As we waited and still no train came in;
But the words of the child in the squalid room
Had spread a glory through the gloom.

An East-End Curate

A SMALL blind street off East Commercial Road;
Window, door; window, door;
Every house like the one before,
Is where the curate, Mr Dowle, has found a pinched abode.
Spectacled, pale, moustache straw-coloured, and with a long
thin face,
Day or dark his lodgings' narrow doorstep does he pace.

A bleached pianoforte, with its drawn silk plaitings faded,
Stands in his room, its keys much yellowed, cyphering, and
abraded,
'Novello's Anthems' lie at hand, and also a few glees,
And 'Laws of Heaven for Earth' in a frame upon the wall one
sees.

He goes through his neighbours' houses as his own, and
   none regards,
And opens their back-doors off-hand, to look for them in
   their yards:
A man is threatening his wife on the other side of the wall,
But the curate lets it pass as knowing the history of it all.

Freely within his hearing the children skip and laugh and
   say:
  'There's Mister Dow-well! There's Mister Dow-well!'
   in their play;
  And the long, pallid, devoted face notes not,
But stoops along abstractedly, for good, or in vain, God wot!

Where They Lived

  DISHEVELLED leaves creep down
  Upon that bank to-day,
 Some green, some yellow, and some pale brown;
  The wet bents bob and sway;
 The once warm slippery turf is sodden
  Where we laughingly sat or lay.

  The summerhouse is gone,
  Leaving a weedy space;
 The bushes that veiled it once have grown
  Gaunt trees that interlace,
 Through whose lank limbs I see too clearly
  The nakedness of the place.

  And where were hills of blue,
  Blind drifts of vapour blow,
 And the names of former dwellers few,
  If any, people know,
 And instead of a voice that called, 'Come in, Dears,'
  Time calls, 'Pass below!'

To C.F.H.

On Her Christening-Day

FAIR Caroline, I wonder what
You think of earth as a dwelling-spot,
And if you'd rather have come, or not?

To-day has laid on you a name
That, though unasked for, you will claim
Lifelong, for love or praise or blame.

May chance and change impose on you
No heavier burthen than this new
Care-chosen one your future through!

Dear stranger here, the prayer is mine
That your experience may combine
Good things with glad. . . . Yes, Caroline!

An Ancient to Ancients

WHERE once we danced, where once we sang,
        Gentlemen,
The floors are sunken, cobwebs hang,
And cracks creep; worms have fed upon
The doors. Yea, sprightlier times were then
Than now, with harps and tabrets gone,
        Gentlemen!

Where once we rowed, where once we sailed,
        Gentlemen,
And damsels took the tiller, veiled
Against too strong a stare (God wot
Their fancy, then or anywhen!)
Upon that shore we are clean forgot,
        Gentlemen!

We have lost somewhat, afar and near,
        Gentlemen,
The thinning of our ranks each year
Affords a hint we are nigh undone,
That we shall not be ever again
The marked of many, loved of one,
        Gentlemen.

In dance the polka hit our wish;
        Gentlemen,
The paced quadrille, the spry schottische,
'Sir Roger'. – And in opera spheres
The 'Girl' (the famed 'Bohemian'),
And 'Trovatore', held the ears,
        Gentlemen.

This season's paintings do not please,
        Gentlemen,
Like Etty, Mulready, Maclise;
Throbbing romance has waned and wanned;
No wizard wields the witching pen
Of Bulwer, Scott, Dumas, and Sand,
        Gentlemen.

The bower we shrined to Tennyson,
        Gentlemen,
Is roof-wrecked; damps there drip upon
Sagged seats, the creeper-nails are rust,
The spider is sole denizen;
Even she who voiced those rhymes is dust,
        Gentlemen!

We who met sunrise sanguine-souled,
        Gentlemen,
Are wearing weary. We are old;
These younger press; we feel our rout
Is imminent to Aïdes' den, –
That evening shades are stretching out,
        Gentlemen!

And yet, though ours be failing frames,
          Gentlemen,
So were some others' history names,
Who trode their track light-limbed and fast
As these youth, and not alien
From enterprise, to their long last,
          Gentlemen.

Sophocles, Plato, Socrates,
          Gentlemen,
Pythagoras, Thucydides,
Herodotus, and Homer, – yea,
Clement, Augustin, Origen,
Burnt brightlier towards their setting-day,
          Gentlemen.

And ye, red-lipped and smooth-browed; list,
          Gentlemen;
Much is there waits you we have missed;
Much lore we leave you worth the knowing,
Much, much has lain outside our ken:
Nay, rush not: time serves: we are going,
          Gentlemen.

Bereft

  IN the black winter morning
No light will be struck near my eyes
While the clock in the stairway is warning
For five, when he used to rise.
          Leave the door unbarred,
          The clock unwound,
          Make my lone bed hard –
          Would 'twere underground!

  When the summer dawns clearly,
And the appletree-tops seem alight,
Who will undraw the curtain and cheerly
Call out that the morning is bright?

When I tarry at market
No form will cross Durnover Lea
In the gathering darkness, to hark at
Grey's Bridge for the pit-pat o' me.

When the supper crock's steaming,
And the time is the time of his tread,
I shall sit by the fire and wait dreaming
In a silence as of the dead.
          Leave the door unbarred,
          The clock unwound,
          Make my lone bed hard –
          Would 'twere underground!

1901

IV Tales Told

San Sebastian

(*August 1813*)

WITH THOUGHTS OF SERGEANT M—— (PENSIONER),
WHO DIED 185–

'WHY, Sergeant, stray on the Ivel Way,
As though at home there were spectres rife?
From first to last 'twas a proud career!
And your sunny years with a gracious wife
     Have brought you a daughter dear.

'I watched her to-day; a more comely maid,
As she danced in her muslin bowed with blue,
Round a Hintock maypole never gayed.'
– 'Aye, aye; I watched her this day, too,
     As it happens,' the Sergeant said.

'My daughter is now,' he again began,
'Of just such an age as one I knew
When we of the Line, the Forlorn-hope van,
On an August morning – a chosen few –
     Stormed San Sebastian.

'She's a score less three; so about was *she* –
The maiden I wronged in Peninsular days. . . .
You may prate of your prowess in lusty times,
But as years gnaw inward you blink your bays,
     And see too well your crimes!

'We'd stormed it at night, by the flapping light
Of burning towers, and the mortar's boom:
We'd topped the breach; but had failed to stay,
For our files were misled by the baffling gloom;
     And we said we'd storm by day.

'So, out of the trenches, with features set,
On that hot, still morning, in measured pace,
Our column climbed; climbed higher yet,
Passed the fauss'bray, scarp, up the curtain-face,
　　And along the parapet.

'From the batteried hornwork the cannoneers
Hove crashing balls of iron fire;
On the shaking gap mount the volunteers
In files, and as they mount expire
　　Amid curses, groans, and cheers.

'Five hours did we storm, five hours re-form,
As Death cooled those hot blood pricked on;
Till our cause was helped by a woe within:
They were blown from the summit we'd leapt upon,
　　And madly we entered in.

'On end for plunder, 'mid rain and thunder
That burst with the lull of our cannonade,
We vamped the streets in the stifling air –
Our hunger unsoothed, our thirst unstayed –
　　And ransacked the buildings there.

'From the shady vaults of their walls of white
We rolled rich puncheons of Spanish grape,
Till at length, with the fire of the wine alight,
I saw at a doorway a fair fresh shape –
　　A woman, a sylph, or sprite.

'Afeard she fled, and with heated head
I pursued to the chamber she called her own;
– When might is right no qualms deter,
And having her helpless and alone
　　I wreaked my will on her.

'She raised her beseeching eyes to me,
And I heard the words of prayer she sent
In her own soft language. . . . Fatefully
I copied those eyes for my punishment
　　In begetting the girl you see!

Till at her room I turned. 'Madam,' I said,
'Have you the wherewithal for this? Pray speak.
Love fills no cupboard. You'll need daily bread.'

'We've nothing, sire,' she lipped; 'and nothing seek.
'Twere base in me to rob my lord unware;
Our hands will earn a pittance week by week.'

And next I saw she had piled her raiment rare
Within the garde-robes, and her household purse,
Her jewels, her least lace of personal wear;

And stood in homespun. Now grown wholly hers,
I handed her the gold, her jewels all,
And him the choicest of her robes diverse.

'I'll take you to the doorway in the wall,
And then adieu,' I told them. 'Friends, withdraw.'
They did so; and she went – beyond recall.

And as I paused beneath the arch I saw
Their moonlit figures – slow, as in surprise –
Descend the slope, and vanish on the haw.

' "Fool," some will say,' I thought. – 'But who is wise,
Save God alone, to weigh my reasons why?'
– 'Hast thou struck home?' came with the boughs' night-sighs.

It was my friend. 'I have struck well. They fly,
But carry wounds that none can cicatrize.'
– 'Not mortal?' said he. 'Lingering – worse,' said I.

The Dance at the Phœnix

To Jenny came a gentle youth
    From inland leazes lone,
His love was fresh as apple-blooth
    By Parrett, Yeo, or Tone.
And duly he entreated her
To be his tender minister,
    And take him for her own.

Now Jenny's life had hardly been
    A life of modesty;
And few in Casterbridge had seen
    More loves of sorts than she
From scarcely sixteen years above;
Among them sundry troopers of
    The King's-Own Cavalry.

But each with charger, sword, and gun,
    Had bluffed the Biscay wave;
And Jenny prized her rural one
    For all the love he gave.
She vowed to be, if they were wed,
His honest wife in heart and head
    From bride-ale hour to grave.

Wedded they were. Her husband's trust
    In Jenny knew no bound,
And Jenny kept her pure and just,
    Till even malice found
No sin or sign of ill to be
In one who walked so decently
    The duteous helpmate's round.

Two sons were born, and bloomed to men,
    And roamed, and were as not:
Alone was Jenny left again
    As ere her mind had sought
A solace in domestic joys,
And ere the vanished pair of boys
    Were sent to sun her cot.

She numbered near on sixty years,
    And passed as elderly,
When, on a day, with flushing fears,
    She learnt from shouts of glee,
And shine of swords, and thump of drum,
Her early loves from war had come,
    The King's-Own Cavalry.

She turned aside, and bowed her head
    Anigh Saint Peter's door;
'Alas for chastened thoughts!' she said;
    'I'm faded now, and hoar,
And yet those notes – they thrill me through,
And those gay forms move me anew
    As they moved me of yore!' . . .

'Twas Christmas, and the Phœnix Inn
    Was lit with tapers tall,
For thirty of the trooper men
    Had vowed to give a ball
As 'Theirs' had done ('twas handed down)
When lying in the selfsame town
    Ere Buonaparté's fall.

That night the throbbing 'Soldier's Joy',
    The measured tread and sway
Of 'Fancy-Lad' and 'Maiden Coy',
    Reached Jenny as she lay
Beside her spouse; till springtide blood
Seemed scouring through her like a flood
    That whisked the years away.

She rose, arrayed, and decked her head
    Where the bleached hairs grew thin;
Upon her cap two bows of red
    She fixed with hasty pin;
Unheard descending to the street
She trod the flags with tune-led feet,
    And stood before the Inn.

Save for the dancers', not a sound
    Disturbed the icy air;
No watchman on his midnight round
    Or traveller was there;
But over All-Saints', high and bright,
Pulsed to the music Sirius white,
    The Wain by Bullstake Square.

She knocked, but found her further stride
     Checked by a sergeant tall:
'Gay Granny, whence come you?' he cried;
     'This is a private ball.'
– 'No one has more right here than me!
Ere you were born, man,' answered she,
     'I knew the regiment all!'

'Take not the lady's visit ill!'
     The steward said; 'for see,
We lack sufficient partners still,
     So, prithee, let her be!'
They seized and whirled her mid the maze,
And Jenny felt as in the days
     Of her immodesty.

Hour chased each hour, and night advanced;
     She sped as shod with wings;
Each time and every time she danced –
     Reels, jigs, poussettes, and flings:
They cheered her as she soared and swooped,
(She had learnt ere art in dancing drooped
     From hops to slothful swings).

The favourite Quick-step 'Speed the Plough' –
     (Cross hands, cast off, and wheel) –
'The Triumph', 'Sylph', 'The Row-dow-dow',
     Famed 'Major Malley's Reel',
'The Duke of York's', 'The Fairy Dance',
'The Bridge of Lodi' (brought from France),
     She beat out, toe and heel.

The 'Fall of Paris' clanged its close,
     And Peter's chime went four,
When Jenny, bosom-beating, rose
     To seek her silent door.
They tiptoed in escorting her,
Lest stroke of heel or clink of spur
     Should break her goodman's snore.

The fire that lately burnt fell slack
    When lone at last was she;
Her nine-and-fifty years came back;
    She sank upon her knee
Beside the durn, and like a dart
A something arrowed through her heart
    In shoots of agony.

Their footsteps died as she leant there,
    Lit by the morning star
Hanging above the moorland, where
    The agèd elm-rows are;
As overnight, from Pummery Ridge
To Maembury Ring and Standfast Bridge
    No life stirred, near or far.

Though inner mischief worked amain,
    She reached her husband's side;
Where, toil-weary, as he had lain
    Beneath the patchwork pied
When forthward yestereve she crept,
And as unwitting, still he slept
    Who did in her confide.

A tear sprang as she turned and viewed
    His features free from guile;
She kissed him long, as when, just wooed,
    She chose his domicile.
She felt she would give more than life
To be the single-hearted wife
    That she had been erstwhile. . . .

Time wore to six. Her husband rose
    And struck the steel and stone;
He glanced at Jenny, whose repose
    Seemed deeper than his own.
With dumb dismay, on closer sight,
He gathered sense that in the night,
    Or morn, her soul had flown.

When told that some too mighty strain
    For one so many-yeared
Had burst her bosom's master-vein,
    His doubts remained unstirred.
His Jenny had not left his side
Betwixt the eve and morning-tide:
    – The King's said not a word.

Well! times are not as times were then,
    Nor fair ones half so free;
And truly they were martial men,
    The King's-Own Cavalry.
And when they went from Casterbridge
And vanished over Mellstock Ridge,
    'Twas saddest morn to see.

The Bride-Night Fire

(*A Wessex Tradition*)

THEY had long met o' Zundays – her true love and she –
    And at junketings, maypoles, and flings;
But she bode wi' a thirtover[1] uncle, and he
Swore by noon and by night that her goodman should be
Naibour Sweatley – a wight often weak at the knee
From taking o' sommat more cheerful than tea –
    Who tranted,[2] and moved people's things.

She cried, 'O pray pity me!' Nought would he hear;
    Then with wild rainy eyes she obeyed.
She chid when her Love was for clinking off wi' her:
The pa'son was told, as the season drew near,
To throw over pu'pit the names of the pair
    As fitting one flesh to be made.

The wedding-day dawned and the morning drew on;
    The couple stood bridegroom and bride;
The evening was passed, and when midnight had gone
The feasters horned,[3] 'God save the King,' and anon
    The pair took their homealong[4] ride.

The lover Tim Tankens mourned heart-sick and leer[5]
   To be thus of his darling deprived:
He roamed in the dark ath'art field, mound, and mere,
And, a'most without knowing it, found himself near
The house of the tranter, and now of his Dear,
   Where the lantern-light showed 'em arrived.

The bride sought her chamber so calm and so pale
   That a Northern had thought her resigned;
But to eyes that had seen her in tidetimes[6] of weal,
Like the white cloud o' smoke, the red battlefield's vail,
   That look spak' of havoc behind.

The bridegroom yet laitered a beaker to drain,
   Then reeled to the linhay[7] for more,
When the candle-snoff kindled some chaff from his grain –
Flames spread, and red vlankers[8] wi' might and wi' main
   Around beams, thatch, and chimley-tun[9] roar.

Young Tim away yond, rafted[10] up by the light,
   Through brimbles and underwood tears,
Till he comes to the orchet, when crooping[11] from sight
In the lewth[12] of a codlin-tree, bivering[13] wi' fright,
Wi' on'y her night-rail to cover her plight,
   His lonesome young Barbree appears.

Her cwold little figure half-naked he views
   Played about by the frolicsome breeze,
Her light-tripping totties,[14] her ten little tooes,
All bare and besprinkled wi' Fall's[15] chilly dews,
While her great gallied[16] eyes through her hair hanging loose
   Shone as stars through a tardle[17] o' trees.

She eyed him; and, as when a weir-hatch is drawn,
   Her tears, penned by terror afore,
With a rushing of sobs in a shower were strawn,
Till her power to pour 'em seemed wasted and gone
   From the heft[18] o' misfortune she bore.

'O Tim, my *own* Tim I must call 'ee – I will!
   All the world has turned round on me so!
Can you help her who loved 'ee, though acting so ill?

Can you pity her misery – feel for her still?
When worse than her body so quivering and chill
  Is her heart in its winter o' woe!

'I think I mid[19] almost ha' borne it,' she said,
  'Had my griefs one by one come to hand;
But O, to be slave to thik husbird,[20] for bread,
And then, upon top o' that, driven to wed,
And then, upon top o' that, burnt out o' bed,
  Is more than my nater can stand!'

Like a lion 'ithin en Tim's spirit outsprung –
(Tim had a great soul when his feelings were wrung) –
  'Feel for 'ee, dear Barbree?' he cried;
And his warm working-jacket then straightway he flung
Round about her, and horsed her by jerks, till she clung
Like a chiel on a gipsy, her figure uphung
  By the sleeves that he tightly had tied.

Over piggeries, and mixens,[21] and apples, and hay,
  They lumpered[22] straight into the night;
And finding ere long where a halter-path[23] lay,
Sighted Tim's house by dawn, on'y seen on their way
By a naibour or two who were up wi' the day,
  But who gathered no clue to the sight.

Then tender Tim Tankens he searched here and there
  For some garment to clothe her fair skin;
But though he had breeches and waistcoats to spare,
He had nothing quite seemly for Barbree to wear,
Who, half shrammed[24] to death, stood and cried on a chair
  At the caddle[25] she found herself in.

There was one thing to do, and that one thing he did,
  He lent her some clothes of his own,
And she took 'em perforce; and while swiftly she slid
Them upon her Tim turned to the winder, as bid,
Thinking, 'O that the picter my duty keeps hid
  To the sight o' my eyes mid[26] be shown!'

In the tallet[27] he stowed her; there huddied[28] she lay,
  Shortening sleeves, legs, and tails to her limbs;
But most o' the time in a mortal bad way,

Well knowing that there'd be the divel to pay
If 'twere found that, instead o' the elements' prey,
   She was living in lodgings at Tim's.

'Where's the tranter?' said men and boys; 'where can he be?'
   'Where's the tranter?' said Barbree alone.
'Where on e'th is the tranter?' said everybod-y:
They sifted the dust of his perished roof-tree,
   And all they could find was a bone.

Then the uncle cried, 'Lord, pray have mercy on me!'
   And in terror began to repent.
But before 'twas complete, and till sure she was free,
Barbree drew up her loft-ladder, tight turned her key –
Tim bringing up breakfast and dinner and tea –
   Till the news of her hiding got vent.

Then followed the custom-kept rout, shout, and flare
Of a skimmity-ride[29] through the naibourhood, ere
   Folk had proof o' wold[30] Sweatley's decay.
Whereupon decent people all stood in a stare,
Saying Tim and his lodger should risk it, and pair:
So he took her to church. An' some laughing lads there
Cried to Tim, 'After Sweatley!' She said, 'I declare
   I stand as a maiden to-day!'

Written 1866; printed 1875

[1] *thirtover*, cross
[2] *tranted*, traded as carrier
[3] *horned*, sang loudly
[4] *homealong*, homeward
[5] *leer*, empty-stomached
[6] *tidetimes*, holidays
[7] *linhay*, lean-to building
[8] *vlankers*, fire-flakes
[9] *chimley-tun*, chimney-stack
[10] *rafted*, roused
[11] *crooping*, squatting down
[12] *lewth*, shelter
[13] *bivering*, with chattering teeth
[14] *totties*, feet
[15] *Fall*, autumn
[16] *gallied*, frightened
[17] *tardle*, entanglement
[18] *heft*, weight
[19] *mid*, might
[20] *thik husbird*, that rascal
[21] *mixens*, manure-heaps
[22] *lumpered*, stumbled
[23] *halter-path*, bridle-path
[24] *shrammed*, numbed
[25] *caddle*, quandary
[26] *mid*, might
[27] *tallet*, loft
[28] *huddied*, hidden
[29] *skimmity-ride*, satirical
   procession with effigies
[30] *wold*, old

A Trampwoman's Tragedy

(*182–*)

I

FROM Wynyard's Gap the livelong day,
       The livelong day,
We beat afoot the northward way
       We had travelled times before.
The sun-blaze burning on our backs,
Our shoulders sticking to our packs,
By fosseway, fields, and turnpike tracks
       We skirted sad Sedge-Moor.

II

Full twenty miles we jaunted on,
       We jaunted on, –
My fancy-man, and jeering John,
       And Mother Lee, and I.
And, as the sun drew down to west,
We climbed the toilsome Poldon crest,
And saw, of landskip sights the best,
       The inn that beamed thereby.

III

For months we had padded side by side,
       Ay, side by side
Through the Great Forest, Blackmoor wide,
       And where the Parret ran.
We'd faced the gusts on Mendip ridge,
Had crossed the Yeo unhelped by bridge,
Been stung by every Marshwood midge,
       I and my fancy-man.

IV

Lone inns we loved, my man and I,
       My man and I;
'King's Stag', 'Windwhistle' high and dry,
       'The Horse' on Hintock Green,

The cosy house at Wynyard's Gap,
'The Hut' renowned on Bredy Knap,
And many another wayside tap
    Where folk might sit unseen.

V

Now as we trudged – O deadly day,
    O deadly day! –
I teased my fancy-man in play
    And wanton idleness.
I walked alongside jeering John,
I laid his hand my waist upon;
I would not bend my glances on
    My lover's dark distress.

VI

Thus Poldon top at last we won,
    At last we won,
And gained the inn at sink of sun
    Far-famed as 'Marshal's Elm'.
Beneath us figured tor and lea,
From Mendip to the western sea –
I doubt if finer sight there be
    Within this royal realm.

VII

Inside the settle all a-row –
    All four a-row
We sat, I next to John, to show
    That he had wooed and won.
And then he took me on his knee,
And swore it was his turn to be
My favoured mate, and Mother Lee
    Passed to my former one.

VIII

Then in a voice I had never heard,
    I had never heard,
My only Love to me: 'One word,
    My lady, if you please!

Whose is the child you are like to bear? –
His? After all my months o' care?'
God knows 'twas not! But, O despair!
    I nodded – still to tease.

IX

Then up he sprung, and with his knife –
    And with his knife
He let out jeering Johnny's life,
    Yes; there, at set of sun.
The slant ray through the window nigh
Gilded John's blood and glazing eye,
Ere scarcely Mother Lee and I
    Knew that the deed was done.

X

The taverns tell the gloomy tale,
    The gloomy tale,
How that at Ivel-chester jail
    My Love, my sweetheart swung;
Though stained till now by no misdeed
Save one horse ta'en in time o' need;
(Blue Jimmy stole right many a steed
    Ere his last fling he flung.)

XI

Thereaft I walked the world alone,
    Alone, alone!
On his death-day I gave my groan
    And dropt his dead-born child.
'Twas nigh the jail, beneath a tree,
None tending me; for Mother Lee
Had died at Glaston, leaving me
    Unfriended on the wild.

XII

And in the night as I lay weak,
    As I lay weak,
The leaves a-falling on my cheek,
    The red moon low declined –

The ghost of him I'd die to kiss
Rose up and said: 'Ah, tell me this!
Was the child mine, or was it his?
    Speak, that I rest may find!'

XIII

O doubt not but I told him then,
    I told him then,
That I had kept me from all men
    Since we joined lips and swore.
Whereat he smiled, and thinned away
As the wind stirred to call up day . . .
– 'Tis past! And here alone I stray
    Haunting the Western Moor.

NOTES. – 'Windwhistle' (Stanza IV). The highness and dryness of Windwhistle Inn was impressed upon the writer two or three years ago, when, after climbing on a hot afternoon to the beautiful spot near which it stands and entering the inn for tea, he was informed by the landlady that none could be had, unless he would fetch water from a valley half a mile off, the house containing not a drop, owing to its situation. However, a tantalizing row of full barrels behind her back testified to a wetness of a certain sort, which was not at that time desired.

'Marshal's Elm' (Stanza VI), so picturesquely situated, is no longer an inn, though the house, or part of it, still remains. It used to exhibit a fine old swinging sign.

'Blue Jimmy' (Stanza X) was a notorious horse-stealer of Wessex in those days, who appropriated more than a hundred horses before he was caught, among others one belonging to a neighbour of the writer's grandfather. He was hanged at the now demolished Ivel-chester or Ilchester jail above mentioned – that building formerly of so many sinister associations in the minds of the local peasantry, and the continual haunt of fever, which at last led to its condemnation.

Its site is now an innocent-looking green meadow.

April 1902

The Ballad of Love's Skeleton

(*179–*)

'COME, let's to Culliford Hill and Wood,
  And watch the squirrels climb,
And look in sunny places there
    For shepherds' thyme.'

– 'Can I have heart for Culliford Wood,
  And hill and bank and tree,
Who know and ponder over all
    Things done by me!'

– 'Then Dear, don hat, and come along:
  We'll strut the Royal strand;
King George has just arrived, his Court,
    His guards, and band.'

– 'You are a Baron of the King's Court
  From Hanover lately come,
And can forget in song and dance
    What chills me numb.

'We'll be the royal scenes for you,
  And band beyond compare,
But how is she who hates her crime
    To frolic there?

'O why did you so urge and say
  'Twould soil your noble name! –
I should have prized a little child,
    And faced the shame.

'I see the child – *that should have been,*
  But was not, born alive;
With such a deed in a woman's life
    A year seems five.

'I asked not for the wifely rank,
  Nor maiden honour saved;
To call a nestling thing my own
    Was all I craved.

'For what's the hurt of shame to one
   Of no more note than me?
Can littlest life beneath the sun
    More littled be?'

— 'Nay, never grieve. The day is bright,
   Just as it was ere then:
In the Assembly Rooms to-night
    Let's joy again!

'The new Quick-Step is the sweetest dance
   For lively toes and heels;
And when we tire of that we'll prance
    Bewitching reels.

'Dear, never grieve! As once we whirled
   So let us whirl to-night,
Forgetting all things save ourselves
    Till dawning light.

'The King and Queen, Princesses three,
   Have promised to meet there
The mayor and townsfolk. I've my card
    And One to spare.

'The Court will dance at the upper end;
   Only a cord between
Them and the burgher-throng below;
    A brilliant scene!'

— 'I'll go. You've still my heart in thrall:
   Save you, all's dark to me.
And God knows what, when love is all,
    The end will be!'

V Presences

In Front of the Landscape

PLUNGING and labouring on in a tide of visions,
  Dolorous and dear,
Forward I pushed my way as amid waste waters
  Stretching around,
Through whose eddies there glimmered the customed
   landscape
  Yonder and near

Blotted to feeble mist. And the coomb and the upland
  Coppice-crowned,
Ancient chalk-pit, milestone, rills in the grass-flat
  Stroked by the light,
Seemed but a ghost-like gauze, and no substantial
  Meadow or mound.

What were the infinite spectacles featuring foremost
  Under my sight,
Hindering me to discern my paced advancement
  Lengthening to miles;
What were the re-creations killing the daytime
  As by the night?

O they were speechful faces, gazing insistent,
  Some as with smiles,
Some as with slow-born tears that brinily trundled
  Over the wrecked
Cheeks that were fair in their flush-time, ash now with
   anguish,
  Harrowed by wiles.

Yes, I could see them, feel them, hear them, address them –
  Halo-bedecked –
And, alas, onwards, shaken by fierce unreason,

Rigid in hate,
Smitten by years-long wryness born of misprision,
Dreaded, suspect.

Then there would breast me shining sights, sweet seasons
Further in date;
Instruments of strings with the tenderest passion
Vibrant, beside
Lamps long extinguished, robes, cheeks, eyes with the
earth's crust
Now corporate.

Also there rose a headland of hoary aspect
Gnawed by the tide,
Frilled by the nimb of the morning as two friends stood there
Guilelessly glad –
Wherefore they knew not – touched by the fringe of an
ecstasy
Scantly descried.

Later images too did the day unfurl me,
Shadowed and sad,
Clay cadavers of those who had shared in the dramas,
Laid now at ease,
Passions all spent, chiefest the one of the broad brow
Sepulture-clad.

So did beset me scenes, miscalled of the bygone,
Over the leaze,
Past the clump, and down to where lay the beheld ones;
– Yea, as the rhyme
Sung by the sea-swell, so in their pleading dumbness
Captured me these.

For, their lost revisiting manifestations
In their live time
Much had I slighted, caring not for their purport,
Seeing behind
Things more coveted, reckoned the better worth calling
Sweet, sad, sublime.

Thus do they now show hourly before the intenser
    Stare of the mind
As they were ghosts avenging their slights by my bypast
    Body-borne eyes,
Show, too, with fuller translation than rested upon them
    As living kind.

Hence wag the tongues of the passing people, saying
    In their surmise,
'Ah – whose is this dull form that perambulates, seeing nought
    Round him that looms
Whithersoever his footsteps turn in his farings,
    Save a few tombs?'

Wessex Heights

(1896)

THERE are some heights in Wessex, shaped as if by a kindly
    hand
For thinking, dreaming, dying on, and at crises when I stand,
Say, on Ingpen Beacon eastward, or on Wylls-Neck
    westwardly,
I seem where I was before my birth, and after death may be.

In the lowlands I have no comrade, not even the lone man's
    friend –
Her who suffereth long and is kind; accepts what he is too
    weak to mend:
Down there they are dubious and askance; there nobody
    thinks as I,
But mind-chains do not clank where one's next neighbour is
    the sky.

In the towns I am tracked by phantoms having weird
    detective ways –
Shadows of beings who fellowed with myself of earlier days:
They hang about at places, and they say harsh heavy things –
Men with a wintry sneer, and women with tart disparagings.

Down there I seem to be false to myself, my simple self that
    was,
And is not now, and I see him watching, wondering what
    crass cause
Can have merged him into such a strange continuator as this,
Who yet has something in common with himself, my
    chrysalis.

I cannot go to the great grey Plain; there's a figure against the
    moon,
Nobody sees it but I, and it makes my breast beat out of tune;
I cannot go to the tall-spired town, being barred by the forms
    now passed
For everybody but me, in whose long vision they stand there
    fast.

There's a ghost at Yell'ham Bottom chiding loud at the fall of
    the night,
There's a ghost in Froom-side Vale, thin-lipped and vague, in
    a shroud of white,
There is one in the railway train whenever I do not want it
    near,
I see its profile against the pane, saying what I would not
    hear.

As for one rare fair woman, I am now but a thought of hers,
I enter her mind and another thought succeeds me that she
    prefers;
Yet my love for her in its fulness she herself even did not
    know;
Well, time cures hearts of tenderness, and now I can let her
    go.

So I am found on Ingpen Beacon, or on Wylls-Neck to the
    west,
Or else on homely Bulbarrow, or little Pilsdon Crest,
Where men have never cared to haunt, nor women have
    walked with me,
And ghosts then keep their distance; and I know some
    liberty.

On a Heath

I COULD hear a gown-skirt rustling
    Before I could see her shape,
Rustling through the heather
    That wove the common's drape,
On that evening of dark weather
    When I hearkened, lips agape.

And the town-shine in the distance
    Did but baffle here the sight,
And then a voice flew forward:
    'Dear, is't you? I fear the night!'
And the herons flapped to norward
    In the firs upon my right.

There was another looming
    Whose life we did not see;
There was one stilly blooming
    Full nigh to where walked we;
There was a shade entombing
    All that was bright of me.

The Place on the Map

I

I LOOK upon the map that hangs by me –
Its shires and towns and rivers lined in varnished artistry –
    And I mark a jutting height
Coloured purple, with a margin of blue sea.

II

– 'Twas a day of latter summer, hot and dry;
Ay, even the waves seemed drying as we walked on, she and I,
    By this spot where, calmly quite,
She unfolded what would happen by and by.

III

This hanging map depicts the coast and place,
And re-creates therewith our unforeboded troublous case
      All distinctly to my sight,
      And her tension, and the aspect of her face.

IV

Weeks and weeks we had loved beneath that blazing blue,
Which had lost the art of raining, as her eyes to-day had too,
      While she told what, as by sleight,
      Shot our firmament with rays of ruddy hue.

V

For the wonder and the wormwood of the whole
Was that what in realms of reason would have joyed our
            double soul
      Wore a torrid tragic light
      Under order-keeping's rigorous control.

VI

So, the map revives her words, the spot, the time,
And the thing we found we had to face before the next
            year's prime;
      The charted coast stares bright,
      And its episode comes back in pantomime.

On an Invitation to the United States

I

My ardours for emprize nigh lost
Since Life has bared its bones to me,
I shrink to seek a modern coast
Whose riper times have yet to be;
Where the new regions claim them free
From that long drip of human tears
Which peoples old in tragedy
Have left upon the centuried years.

II

For, wonning in these ancient lands,
Enchased and lettered as a tomb,
And scored with prints of perished hands,
And chronicled with dates of doom,
Though my own Being bear no bloom
I trace the lives such scenes enshrine,
Give past exemplars present room,
And their experience count as mine.

Rome

The Vatican: Sala delle Muse

(*1887*)

I SAT in the Muses' Hall at the mid of the day,
And it seemed to grow still, and the people to pass away,
And the chiselled shapes to combine in a haze of sun,
Till beside a Carrara column there gleamed forth One.

She looked not this nor that of those beings divine,
But each and the whole – an essence of all the Nine;
With tentative foot she neared to my halting-place,
A pensive smile on her sweet, small, marvellous face.

'Regarded so long, we render thee sad?' said she.
'Not you,' sighed I, 'but my own inconstancy!
I worship each and each; in the morning one,
And then, alas! another at sink of sun.

'To-day my soul clasps Form; but where is my troth
Of yesternight with Tune: can one cleave to both?'
– 'Be not perturbed,' said she. 'Though apart in fame,
As I and my sisters are one, those, too, are the same.'

– 'But my love goes further – to Story, and Dance, and Hymn,
The lover of all in a sun-sweep is fool to whim –
Is swayed like a river-weed as the ripples run!'
– 'Nay, wooer, thou sway'st not. These are but phases of one;

'And that one is I; and I am projected from thee,
One that out of thy brain and heart thou causest to be –
Extern to thee nothing. Grieve not, nor thyself becall,
Woo where thou wilt; and rejoice thou canst love at all!'

Rome

*At the Pyramid of Cestius near the
Graves of Shelley and Keats*

(*1887*)

WHO, then, was Cestius,
        And what is he to me? –
Amid thick thoughts and memories multitudinous
        One thought alone brings he.

    I can recall no word
        Of anything he did;
For me he is a man who died and was interred
        To leave a pyramid

    Whose purpose was exprest
        Not with its first design,
Nor till, far down in Time, beside it found their rest
        Two countrymen of mine.

    Cestius in life, maybe,
        Slew, breathed out threatening;
I know not. This I know: in death all silently
        He does a finer thing,

    In beckoning pilgrim feet
        With marble finger high
To where, by shadowy wall and history-haunted street,
        Those matchless singers lie. . . .

       – Say, then, he lived and died
     That stones which bear his name
Should mark, through Time, where two immortal Shades
         abide;
     It is an ample fame.

At Lulworth Cove a Century Back

HAD I but lived a hundred years ago
I might have gone, as I have gone this year,
By Warmwell Cross on to a Cove I know,
And Time have placed his finger on me there:

'You see that man?' – I might have looked, and said,
'O yes: I see him. One that boat has brought
Which dropped down Channel round Saint Alban's Head.
So commonplace a youth calls not my thought.'

'You see that man?' – 'Why yes; I told you; yes:
Of an idling town-sort; thin; hair brown in hue;
And as the evening light scants less and less
He looks up at a star, as many do.'

'You see that man?' – 'Nay, leave me!' then I plead,
'I have fifteen miles to vamp across the lea,
And it grows dark, and I am weary-kneed:
I have said the third time; yes, that man I see!'

'Good. That man goes to Rome – to death, despair;
And no one notes him now but you and I:
A hundred years, and the world will follow him there,
And bend with reverence where his ashes lie.'

September 1920

NOTE. – In September 1820 Keats, on his way to Rome, landed
one day on the Dorset coast, and composed the sonnet, 'Bright
Star! would I were steadfast as thou art.' The spot of his landing is
judged to have been Lulworth Cove.

Lausanne

In Gibbon's Old Garden: 11–12 p.m.

27 June 1897

*(The 110th anniversary of the completion of the 'Decline and Fall' at the
same hour and place)*

A SPIRIT seems to pass,
 Formal in pose, but grave withal and grand:
 He contemplates a volume in his hand,
And far lamps fleck him through the thin acacias.

 Anon the book is closed,
 With 'It is finished!' And at the alley's end
 He turns, and when on me his glances bend
As from the Past comes speech – small, muted, yet composed.

 'How fares the Truth now? – Ill?
 – Do pens but slily further her advance?
 May one not speed her but in phrase askance?
Do scribes aver the Comic to be Reverend still?

 'Still rule those minds on earth
 At whom sage Milton's wormwood words were hurled:
 ''Truth like a bastard comes into the world
Never without ill-fame to him who gives her birth''?'

Zermatt

To the Matterhorn

(June–July 1897)

THIRTY-TWO years since, up against the sun,
Seven shapes, thin atomies to lower sight,
Labouringly leapt and gained thy gabled height,
And four lives paid for what the seven had won.

They were the first by whom the deed was done,
And when I look at thee, my mind takes flight
To that day's tragic feat of manly might,
As though, till then, of history thou hadst none.

Yet ages ere men topped thee, late and soon
Thou didst behold the planets lift and lower;
Saw'st, maybe, Joshua's pausing sun and moon,
And the betokening sky when Cæsar's power
Approached its bloody end; yea, even that Noon
When darkness filled the earth till the ninth hour.

Night in the Old Home

WHEN the wasting embers redden the chimney-breast,
And Life's bare pathway looms like a desert track to me,
And from hall and parlour the living have gone to their rest,
My perished people who housed them here come back to
     me.

They come and seat them around in their mouldy places,
Now and then bending towards me a glance of wistfulness,
A strange upbraiding smile upon all their faces,
And in the bearing of each a passive tristfulness.

'Do you uphold me, lingering and languishing here,
A pale late plant of your once strong stock?' I say to them;
'A thinker of crooked thoughts upon Life in the sere,
And on That which consigns men to night after showing the
     day to them?'

' – O let be the Wherefore! We fevered our years not thus:
Take of Life what it grants, without question!' they answer
     me seemingly.
'Enjoy, suffer, wait: spread the table here freely like us,
And, satisfied, placid, unfretting, watch Time away
     beamingly!'

Old Furniture

I KNOW not how it may be with others
    Who sit amid relics of householdry
That date from the days of their mothers' mothers,
    But well I know how it is with me
        Continually.

I see the hands of the generations
    That owned each shiny familiar thing
In play on its knobs and indentations,
    And with its ancient fashioning
        Still dallying:

Hands behind hands, growing paler and paler,
    As in a mirror a candle-flame
Shows images of itself, each frailer
    As it recedes, though the eye may frame
        Its shape the same.

On the clock's dull dial a foggy finger,
    Moving to set the minutes right
With tentative touches that lift and linger
    In the wont of a moth on a summer night,
        Creeps to my sight.

On this old viol, too, fingers are dancing –
    As whilom – just over the strings by the nut,
The tip of a bow receding, advancing
    In airy quivers, as if it would cut
        The plaintive gut.

And I see a face by that box for tinder,
    Glowing forth in fits from the dark,
And fading again, as the linten cinder
    Kindles to red at the flinty spark,
        Or goes out stark.

Well, well. It is best to be up and doing,
    The world has no use for one to-day
Who eyes things thus – no aim pursuing!
    He should not continue in this stay,
        But sink away.

Family Portraits

THREE picture-drawn people stepped out of their frames –
'The blast, how it blew!
And the white-shrouded candles flapped smoke-headed
flames;
– Three picture-drawn people came down from their frames,
And dumbly in lippings they told me their names,
Full well though I knew.

The first was a maiden of mild wistful tone,
Gone silent for years,
The next a dark woman in former time known;
But the first one, the maiden of mild wistful tone,
So wondering, unpractised, so vague and alone,
Nigh moved me to tears.

The third was a sad man – a man of much gloom;
And before me they passed
In the shade of the night, at the back of the room,
The dark and fair woman, the man of much gloom,
Three persons, in far-off years forceful, but whom
Death now fettered fast.

They set about acting some drama, obscure,
The women and he,
With puppet-like movements of mute strange allure;
Yea, set about acting some drama, obscure,
Till I saw 'twas their own lifetime's tragic amour,
Whose course begot me;

Yea – a mystery, ancestral, long hid from my reach
In the perished years past,
That had mounted to dark doings each against each
In those ancestors' days, and long hid from my reach;
Which their restless enghostings, it seemed, were to teach
Me in full, at this last.

But fear fell upon me like frost, of some hurt
    If they entered anew
On the orbits they smartly had swept when expert
In the law-lacking passions of life, – of some hurt
To their souls – and thus mine – which I fain would avert;
    So, in sweat cold as dew,

'Why wake up all this?' I cried out. 'Now, so late!
    Let old ghosts be laid!'
And they stiffened, drew back to their frames and numb
    state,
Gibbering: 'Thus are your own ways to shape, know too
    late!'
Then I grieved that I'd not had the courage to wait
    And see the play played.

I have grieved ever since: to have balked future pain,
    My blood's tendance foreknown,
Had been triumph. Nights long stretched awake I have lain
Perplexed in endeavours to balk future pain
By uncovering the drift of their drama. In vain,
    Though therein lay my own.

The Sunshade

    AH – it's the skeleton of a lady's sunshade,
        Here at my feet in the hard rock's chink,
        Merely a naked sheaf of wires! –
        Twenty years have gone with their livers and diers
        Since it was silked in its white or pink.

    Noonshine riddles the ribs of the sunshade,
        No more a screen from the weakest ray;
        Nothing to tell us the hue of its dyes,
        Nothing but rusty bones as it lies
        In its coffin of stone, unseen till to-day.

Where is the woman who carried that sunshade
Up and down this seaside place? –
Little thumb standing against its stem,
Thoughts perhaps bent on a love-stratagem,
Softening yet more the already soft face!

Is the fair woman who carried that sunshade
A skeleton just as her property is,
Laid in the chink that none may scan?
And does she regret – if regret dust can –
The vain things thought when she flourished this?

Swanage Cliffs

At Casterbridge Fair

II. *Former Beauties*

THESE market-dames, mid-aged, with lips thin-drawn,
    And tissues sere,
Are they the ones we loved in years agone,
    And courted here?

Are these the muslined pink young things to whom
    We vowed and swore
In nooks on summer Sundays by the Froom,
    Or Budmouth shore?

Do they remember those gay tunes we trod
    Clasped on the green;
Aye; trod till moonlight set on the beaten sod
    A satin sheen?

They must forget, forget! They cannot know
    What once they were,
Or memory would transfigure them, and show
    Them always fair.

VII. *After the Fair*

THE singers are gone from the Cornmarket-place
    With their broadsheets of rhymes,
The street rings no longer in treble and bass
    With their skits on the times,
And the Cross, lately thronged, is a dim naked space
    That but echoes the stammering chimes.

From Clock-corner steps, as each quarter ding-dongs,
    Away the folk roam
By the 'Hart' and Grey's Bridge into byways and 'drongs',
    Or across the ridged loam;
The younger ones shrilling the lately heard songs,
    The old saying, 'Would we were home.'

The shy-seeming maiden so mute in the fair
    Now rattles and talks,
And that one who looked the most swaggering there
    Grows sad as she walks,
And she who seemed eaten by cankering care
    In statuesque sturdiness stalks.

And midnight clears High Street of all but the ghosts
    Of its buried burghees,
From the latest far back to those old Roman hosts
    Whose remains one yet sees,
Who loved, laughed, and fought, hailed their friends, drank
        their toasts
  At their meeting-times here, just as these!

1902

NOTE. – 'The chimes' (line 6) will be listened for in vain here at
midnight now, having been abolished some years ago.

She Hears the Storm

THERE was a time in former years –
    While my roof-tree was his –
When I should have been distressed by fears
    At such a night as this!

I should have murmured anxiously,
    'The pricking rain strikes cold;
His road is bare of hedge or tree,
    And he is getting old.'

But now the fitful chimney-roar,
    The drone of Thorncombe trees,
The Froom in flood upon the moor,
    The mud of Mellstock Leaze,

The candle slanting sooty-wick'd,
    The thuds upon the thatch,
The eaves-drops on the window flicked,
    The clacking garden-hatch,

And what they mean to wayfarers,
    I scarcely heed or mind;
He has won that storm-tight roof of hers
    Which Earth grants all her kind.

A Wife Comes Back

THIS is the story a man told me
Of his life's one day of dreamery.

    A woman came into his room
Between the dawn and the creeping day:
She was the years-wed wife from whom
He had parted, and who lived far away,
    As if strangers they.

He wondered, and as she stood
She put on youth in her look and air,
And more was he wonderstruck as he viewed
Her form and flesh bloom yet more fair
    While he watched her there;

Till she freshed to the pink and brown
That were hers on the night when first they met,
When she was the charm of the idle town,
And he the pick of the club-fire set. . . .
    His eyes grew wet,

And he stretched his arms: 'Stay – rest! – '
He cried. 'Abide with me so, my own!'
But his arms closed in on his hard bare breast;
She had vanished with all he had looked upon
    Of her beauty: gone.

He clothed, and drew downstairs,
But she was not in the house, he found;
And he passed out under the leafy pairs
Of the avenue elms, and searched around
    To the park-pale bound.

He mounted, and rode till night
To the city to which she had long withdrawn,
The vision he bore all day in his sight
Being her young self as pondered on
    In the dim of dawn.

' – The lady here long ago –
Is she now here? – young – or such age as she is?'
' – She is still here.' – 'Thank God. Let her know;
She'll pardon a comer so late as this
    Whom she'd fain not miss.'

She received him – an ancient dame,
Who hemmed, with features frozen and numb,
'How strange! – I'd almost forgotten your name! –
A call just now – is troublesome;
    Why did you come?'

The House of Hospitalities

HERE we broached the Christmas barrel,
  Pushed up the charred log-ends;
Here we sang the Christmas carol,
  And called in friends.

Time has tired me since we met here
  When the folk now dead were young,
Since the viands were outset here
  And quaint songs sung.

And the worm has bored the viol
  That used to lead the tune,
Rust eaten out the dial
  That struck night's noon.

Now no Christmas brings in neighbours,
  And the New Year comes unlit;
Where we sang the mole now labours,
  And spiders knit.

Yet at midnight if here walking,
  When the moon sheets wall and tree,
I see forms of old time talking,
  Who smile on me.

Heredity

I AM the family face;
Flesh perishes, I live on,
Projecting trait and trace
Through time to times anon,
And leaping from place to place
Over oblivion.

The years-heired feature that can
In curve and voice and eye
Despise the human span
Of durance – that is I;
The eternal thing in man,
That heeds no call to die.

The Pedigree

I

I BENT in the deep of night
Over a pedigree the chronicler gave
As mine; and as I bent there, half-unrobed,
The uncurtained panes of my window-square let in the
    watery light
Of the moon in its old age:
And green-rheumed clouds were hurrying past where mute
    and cold it globed
Like a drifting dolphin's eye seen through a lapping wave.

II

So, scanning my sire-sown tree,
And the hieroglyphs of this spouse tied to that,
With offspring mapped below in lineage,
    Till the tangles troubled me,
The branches seemed to twist into a seared and cynic face
    Which winked and tokened towards the window like a
        Mage
Enchanting me to gaze again thereat.

III

It was a mirror now,
And in it a long perspective I could trace
Of my begetters, dwindling backward each past each
    All with the kindred look,
    Whose names had since been inked down in their place
        On the recorder's book,
Generation and generation of my mien, and build, and brow.

IV

And then did I divine
That every heave and coil and move I made
Within my brain, and in my mood and speech,
Was in the glass portrayed
As long forestalled by their so making it;
The first of them, the primest fuglemen of my line,
Being fogged in far antiqueness past surmise and reason's
reach.

V

Said I then, sunk in tone,
'I am merest mimicker and counterfeit! –
Though thinking, *I am I,
And what I do I do myself alone.*'
– The cynic twist of the page thereat unknit
Back to its normal figure, having wrought its purport wry,
The Mage's mirror left the window-square,
And the stained moon and drift retook their places there.

1916

His Immortality

I

I SAW a dead man's finer part
Shining within each faithful heart
Of those bereft. Then said I: 'This must be
His immortality.'

II

I looked there as the seasons wore,
And still his soul continuously bore
A life in theirs. But less its shine excelled
Than when I first beheld.

III

His fellow-yearsmen passed, and then
In later hearts I looked for him again;
And found him – shrunk, alas! into a thin
        And spectral mannikin.

IV

Lastly I ask – now old and chill –
If aught of him remain unperished still;
And find, in me alone, a feeble spark,
        Dying amid the dark.

February 1899

The Superseded

I

As newer comers crowd the fore,
        We drop behind.
– We who have laboured long and sore
        Times out of mind,
And keen are yet, must not regret
        To drop behind.

II

Yet there are some of us who grieve
        To go behind;
Staunch, strenuous souls who scarce believe
        Their fires declined,
And know none spares, remembers, cares
        Who go behind.

III

'Tis not that we have unforetold
        The drop behind;
We feel the new must oust the old
        In every kind;

But yet we think, must we, must *we*,
Too, drop behind?

Beyond the Last Lamp

(*Near Tooting Common*)

I

WHILE rain, with eve in partnership,
Descended darkly, drip, drip, drip,
Beyond the last lone lamp I passed
    Walking slowly, whispering sadly,
    Two linked loiterers, wan, downcast:
Some heavy thought constrained each face,
And blinded them to time and place.

II

The pair seemed lovers, yet absorbed
In mental scenes no longer orbed
By love's young rays. Each countenance
    As it slowly, as it sadly
    Caught the lamplight's yellow glance,
Held in suspense a misery
At things which had been or might be.

III

When I retrod that watery way
Some hours beyond the droop of day,
Still I found pacing there the twain
    Just as slowly, just as sadly,
    Heedless of the night and rain.
One could but wonder who they were
And what wild woe detained them there.

IV

Though thirty years of blur and blot
Have slid since I beheld that spot,
And saw in curious converse there
    Moving slowly, moving sadly
    That mysterious tragic pair,
Its olden look may linger on –
All but the couple; they have gone.

V

Whither? Who knows, indeed. . . . And yet
To me, when nights are weird and wet,
Without those comrades there at tryst
    Creeping slowly, creeping sadly,
    That lone lane does not exist.
There they seem brooding on their pain,
And will, while such a lane remain.

Friends Beyond

WILLIAM DEWY, Tranter Reuben, Farmer Ledlow late at
    plough,
    Robert's kin, and John's, and Ned's,
And the Squire, and Lady Susan, lie in Mellstock churchyard
    now!

'Gone,' I call them, gone for good, that group of local hearts
    and heads;
    Yet at mothy curfew-tide,
And at midnight when the noon-heat breathes it back from
    walls and leads,

They've a way of whispering to me – fellow-wight who yet
    abide –
    In the muted, measured note
Of a ripple under archways, or a lone cave's stillicide:

'We have triumphed: this achievement turns the bane to
   antidote,
      Unsuccesses to success,
Many thought-worn eves and morrows to a morrow free of
   thought.

'No more need we corn and clothing, feel of old terrestrial
   stress;
      Chill detraction stirs no sigh;
Fear of death has even bygone us: death gave all that we
   possess.'

W.D. – 'Ye mid burn the old bass-viol that I set such value by.'
Squire. – 'You may hold the manse in fee,
      You may wed my spouse, may let my children's
         memory of me die.'

Lady S. – 'You may have my rich brocades, my laces; take
      each household key;
         Ransack coffer, desk, bureau;
      Quiz the few poor treasures hid there, con the letters
         kept by me.'

Far. – 'Ye mid zell my favourite heifer, ye mid let the charlock
   grow,
      Foul the grinterns, give up thrift.'
Far. Wife. – 'If ye break my best blue china, children, I shan't
   care or ho.'

All. – 'We've no wish to hear the tidings, how the people's
   fortunes shift;
      What your daily doings are;
      Who are wedded, born, divided; if your lives beat slow
         or swift.

'Curious not the least are we if our intents you make or mar,
      If you quire to our old tune,
If the City stage still passes, if the weirs still roar afar.'

– Thus, with very gods' composure, freed those crosses late
    and soon
        Which, in life, the Trine allow
(Why, none witteth), and ignoring all that haps beneath the
    moon,

William Dewy, Tranter Reuben, Farmer Ledlow late at
    plough,
        Robert's kin, and John's, and Ned's,
And the Squire, and Lady Susan, murmur mildly to me now.

Transformations

PORTION of this yew
Is a man my grandsire knew,
Bosomed here at its foot:
This branch may be his wife,
A ruddy human life
Now turned to a green shoot.

These grasses must be made
Of her who often prayed,
Last century, for repose;
And the fair girl long ago
Whom I often tried to know
May be entering this rose.

So, they are not underground,
But as nerves and veins abound
In the growths of upper air,
And they feel the sun and rain,
And the energy again
That made them what they were!

The Choirmaster's Burial

HE often would ask us
That, when he died,
After playing so many
To their last rest,
If out of us any
Should here abide,
And it would not task us,
We would with our lutes
Play over him
By his grave-brim
The psalm he liked best –
The one whose sense suits
'Mount Ephraim' –
And perhaps we should seem
To him, in Death's dream,
Like the seraphim.

As soon as I knew
That his spirit was gone
I thought this his due,
And spoke thereupon.

'I think,' said the vicar,
'A read service quicker
Than viols out-of-doors
In these frosts and hoars.
That old-fashioned way
Requires a fine day,
And it seems to me
It had better not be.'

Hence, that afternoon,
Though never knew he
That his wish could not be,
To get through it faster
They buried the master
Without any tune.

But 'twas said that, when
At the dead of next night

The vicar looked out,
There struck on his ken
Thronged roundabout,
Where the frost was graying
The headstoned grass,
A band all in white
Like the saints in church-glass,
Singing and playing
The ancient stave
By the choirmaster's grave.

Such the tenor man told
When he had grown old.

Voices from Things Growing in a Churchyard

THESE flowers are I, poor Fanny Hurd,
      Sir or Madam,
A little girl here sepultured.
Once I flit-fluttered like a bird
Above the grass, as now I wave
In daisy shapes above my grave,
      All day cheerily,
      All night eerily!

– I am one Bachelor Bowring, 'Gent',
      Sir or Madam;
In shingled oak my bones were pent;
Hence more than a hundred years I spent
In my feat of change from a coffin-thrall
To a dancer in green as leaves on a wall,
      All day cheerily,
      All night eerily!

– I, these berries of juice and gloss,
      Sir or Madam,
Am clean forgotten as Thomas Voss;
Thin-urned, I have burrowed away from the moss
That covers my sod, and have entered this yew,

And turned to clusters ruddy of view,
          All day cheerily,
          All night eerily!

– The Lady Gertrude, proud, high-bred,
          Sir or Madam,
Am I – this laurel that shades your head;
Into its veins I have stilly sped,
And made them of me; and my leaves now shine,
As did my satins superfine,
          All day cheerily,
          All night eerily!

– I, who as innocent withwind climb,
          Sir or Madam,
Am one Eve Greensleeves, in olden time
Kissed by men from many a clime,
Beneath sun, stars, in blaze, in breeze,
As now by glowworms and by bees,
          All day cheerily,
          All night eerily![1]

– I'm old Squire Audeley Grey, who grew,
          Sir or Madam,
Aweary of life, and in scorn withdrew;
Till anon I clambered up anew
As ivy-green, when my ache was stayed,
And in that attire I have longtime gayed
          All day cheerily,
          All night eerily!

– And so these maskers breathe to each
          Sir or Madam
Who lingers there, and their lively speech
Affords an interpreter much to teach,
As their murmurous accents seem to come
Thence hitheraround in a radiant hum,
          All day cheerily,
          All night eerily!

[1] It was said her real name was Eve Trevillian or Trevelyan; and that she was the handsome mother of two or three illegitimate children, *circa* 1784–95.

While Drawing in a Churchyard

'IT is sad that so many of worth,
　　Still in the flesh,' soughed the yew,
'Misjudge their lot whom kindly earth
　　　　Secludes from view.

'They ride their diurnal round
　　Each day-span's sum of hours
In peerless ease, without jolt or bound
　　　　Or ache like ours.

'If the living could but hear
　　What is heard by my roots as they creep
Round the restful flock, and the things said there,
　　　　No one would weep.'

' "Now set among the wise,"
　　They say: "Enlarged in scope,
That no God trumpet us to rise
　　　　We truly hope." '

I listened to his strange tale
　　In the mood that stillness brings,
And I grew to accept as the day wore pale
　　　　That show of things.

A Spellbound Palace

(Hampton Court)

ON this kindly yellow day of mild low-travelling winter sun
　　　　The stirless depths of the yews
　　　　Are vague with misty blues:
Across the spacious pathways stretching spires of shadow
　　run,
And the wind-gnawed walls of ancient brick are fired
　　vermilion.

Two or three early sanguine finches tune
  Some tentative strains, to be enlarged by May or June:
      From a thrush or blackbird
      Comes now and then a word,
While an enfeebled fountain somewhere within is heard.

      Our footsteps wait awhile,
      Then draw beneath the pile,
      When an inner court outspreads
      As 'twere History's own asile,
Where the now-visioned fountain its attenuate crystal sheds
In passive lapse that seems to ignore the yon world's
    clamorous clutch,
And lays an insistent numbness on the place, like a cold
    hand's touch.

And there swaggers the Shade of a straddling King, plumed,
    sworded, with sensual face,
And lo, too, that of his Minister, at a bold self-centred pace:
Sheer in the sun they pass; and thereupon all is still,
Save the mindless fountain tinkling on with thin enfeebled
    will.

In a Cathedral City

    THESE people have not heard your name;
    No loungers in this placid place
    Have helped to bruit your beauty's fame.

    The grey Cathedral, towards whose face
    Bend eyes untold, has met not yours;
    Your shade has never swept its base,

    Your form has never darked its doors,
    Nor have your faultless feet once thrown
    A pensive pit-pat on its floors.

    Along the street to maids well known
    Blithe lovers hum their tender airs,
    But in your praise voice not a tone. . . .

– Since nought bespeaks you here, or bears,
As I, your imprint through and through,
Here might I rest, till my heart shares
The spot's unconsciousness of you!

Salisbury

In a Museum

I

HERE'S the mould of a musical bird long passed from light,
Which over the earth before man came was winging;
There's a contralto voice I heard last night,
That lodges in me still with its sweet singing.

II

Such a dream is Time that the coo of this ancient bird
Has perished not, but is blent, or will be blending
Mid visionless wilds of space with the voice that I heard,
In the full-fugued song of the universe unending.

Exeter

In a Whispering Gallery

THAT whisper takes the voice
Of a Spirit's compassionings,
Close, but invisible,
And throws me under a spell
At the kindling vision it brings;
And for a moment I rejoice,
And believe in transcendent things
That would mould from this muddy earth
A spot for the splendid birth
Of everlasting lives,
Whereto no night arrives;

And this gaunt gray gallery
A tabernacle of worth
On this drab-aired afternoon,
When you can barely see
Across its hazed lacune
If opposite aught there be
Of fleshed humanity
Wherewith I may commune;
Or if the voice so near
Be a soul's voice floating here.

The Background and the Figure

(*Lover's Ditty*)

I THINK of the slope where the rabbits fed,
    Of the periwinks' rockwork lair,
Of the fuchsias ringing their bells of red –
    And the something else seen there.

Between the blooms where the sod basked bright,
    By the bobbing fuchsia trees,
Was another and yet more eyesome sight –
    The sight that richened these.

I shall seek those beauties in the spring,
    When the days are fit and fair,
But only as foils to the one more thing
    That also will flower there!

Near Lanivet, 1872

THERE was a stunted handpost just on the crest,
    Only a few feet high:
She was tired, and we stopped in the twilight-time for her
        rest,
    At the crossways close thereby.

She leant back, being so weary, against its stem,
    And laid her arms on its own,
Each open palm stretched out to each end of them,
    Her sad face sideways thrown.

Her white-clothed form at this dim-lit cease of day
    Made her look as one crucified
In my gaze at her from the midst of the dusty way,
    And hurriedly 'Don't,' I cried.

I do not think she heard. Loosing thence she said,
    As she stepped forth ready to go,
'I am rested now. – Something strange came into my head;
    I wish I had not leant so!'

And wordless we moved onward down from the hill
    In the west cloud's murked obscure,
And looking back we could see the handpost still
    In the solitude of the moor.

'It struck her too,' I thought, for as if afraid
    She heavily breathed as we trailed;
Till she said, 'I did not think how 'twould look in the shade,
    When I leant there like one nailed.'

I, lightly: 'There's nothing in it. For *you*, anyhow!'
    – 'O I know there is not,' said she . . .
'Yet I wonder . . . If no one is bodily crucified now,
    In spirit one may be!'

And we dragged on and on, while we seemed to see
    In the running of Time's far glass
Her crucified, as she had wondered if she might be
    Some day. – Alas, alas!

'In the Seventies'

'Qui deridetur ab amico suo sicut ego.' – JOB

IN the seventies I was bearing in my breast,
          Penned tight,
Certain starry thoughts that threw a magic light
On the worktimes and the soundless hours of rest
In the seventies; aye, I bore them in my breast
          Penned tight.

In the seventies when my neighbours – even my friend –
          Saw me pass,
Heads were shaken, and I heard the words, 'Alas,
For his onward years and name unless he mend!'
In the seventies, when my neighbours and my friend
          Saw me pass.

In the seventies those who met me did not know
          Of the vision
That immuned me from the chillings of misprision
And the damps that choked my goings to and fro
In the seventies; yea, those nodders did not know
          Of the vision.

In the seventies nought could darken or destroy it,
          Locked in me,
Though as delicate as lamp-worm's lucency;
Neither mist nor murk could weaken or alloy it
In the seventies! – could not darken or destroy it,
          Locked in me.

Exeunt Omnes

I

EVERYBODY else, then, going,
And I still left where the fair was? . . .
Much have I seen of neighbour loungers
    Making a lusty showing,
    Each now past all knowing.

II

There is an air of blankness
In the street and the littered spaces;
Thoroughfare, steeple, bridge and highway
    Wizen themselves to lankness;
    Kennels dribble dankness.

III

Folk all fade. And whither,
As I wait alone where the fair was?
Into the clammy and numbing night-fog
    Whence they entered hither.
    Soon one more goes thither!

2 June 1913

'Who's in the Next Room?'

'WHO'S in the next room? – who?
    I seemed to see
Somebody in the dawning passing through,
    Unknown to me.'
'Nay: you saw nought. He passed invisibly.'

'Who's in the next room? – who?
    I seem to hear
Somebody muttering firm in a language new
    That chills the ear.'
'No: you catch not his tongue who has entered there.'

'Who's in the next room? – who?
    I seem to feel
His breath like a clammy draught, as if it drew
    From the Polar Wheel.'
'No: none who breathes at all does the door conceal.'

'Who's in the next room? – who?
    A figure wan
With a message to one in there of something due?
    Shall I know him anon?'
'Yea he; and he brought such; and you'll know him anon.'

VI Selves Unseeing

After a Romantic Day

THE railway bore him through
An earthen cutting out from a city:
    There was no scope for view,
Though the frail light shed by a slim young moon
    Fell like a friendly tune.

    Fell like a liquid ditty,
And the blank lack of any charm
    Of landscape did no harm.
The bald steep cutting, rigid, rough,
    And moon-lit, was enough
For poetry of place: its weathered face
Formed a convenient sheet whereon
The visions of his mind were drawn.

After the Burial

THE family had buried him,
    Their bread-bringer, their best:
They had returned to the house, whose hush a dim
    Vague vacancy expressed.

There sat his sons, mute, rigid-faced,
    His daughters, strained, red-eyed,
His wife, whose wan, worn features, vigil-traced,
    Bent over him when he died.

At once a peal bursts from the bells
    Of a large tall tower hard by:
Along the street the jocund clangour swells,
    And upward to the sky.

Probably it was a wedding-peal,
     Or possibly for a birth,
Or townsman knighted for political zeal,
     This resonant mark of mirth.

The mourners, heavy-browed, sat on
     Motionless. Well they heard,
They could not help it; nevertheless thereon
     Spoke not a single word,

Nor window did they close, to numb
     The bells' insistent calls
Of joy; but suffered the harassing din to come
     And penetrate their souls.

Heiress and Architect

For A. W. Blomfield

SHE sought the Studios, beckoning to her side
An arch-designer, for she planned to build.
He was of wise contrivance, deeply skilled
In every intervolve of high and wide –
     Well fit to be her guide.

     'Whatever it be,'
     Responded he,
With cold, clear voice, and cold, clear view,
'In true accord with prudent fashionings
For such vicissitudes as living brings,
And thwarting not the law of stable things,
     That will I do.'

'Shape me,' she said, 'high halls with tracery
And open ogive-work, that scent and hue
Of buds, and travelling bees, may come in through,
The note of birds, and singings of the sea,
     For these are much to me.'

'An idle whim!'
Broke forth from him
Whom nought could warm to gallantries:
'Cede all these buds and birds, the zephyr's call,
And scents, and hues, and things that falter all,
And choose as best the close and surly wall,
For winters freeze.'

'Then frame,' she cried, 'wide fronts of crystal glass,
That I may show my laughter and my light –
Light like the sun's by day, the stars' by night –
Till rival heart-queens, envying, wail, "Alas,
Her glory!" as they pass.'

'O maid misled!'
He sternly said
Whose facile foresight pierced her dire;
'Where shall abide the soul when, sick of glee,
It shrinks, and hides, and prays no eye may see?
Those house them best who house for secrecy,
For you will tire.'

'A little chamber, then, with swan and dove
Ranged thickly, and engrailed with rare device
Of reds and purples, for a Paradise
Wherein my Love may greet me, I my Love,
When he shall know thereof?'

'This, too, is ill,'
He answered still,
The man who swayed her like a shade.
'An hour will come when sight of such sweet nook
Would bring a bitterness too sharp to brook,
When brighter eyes have won away his look;
For you will fade.'

Then said she faintly: 'O, contrive some way –
Some narrow winding turret, quite mine own,
To reach a loft where I may grieve alone!
It is a slight thing; hence do not, I pray,
This last dear fancy slay!'

'Such winding ways
        Fit not your days,'
Said he, the man of measuring eye;
'I must even fashion as the rule declares,
To wit: Give space (since life ends unawares)
To hale a coffined corpse adown the stairs;
        For you will die.'

1867. 8 Adelphi Terrace

Lines

To a Movement in Mozart's E-Flat Symphony

SHOW me again the time
    When in the Junetide's prime
We flew by meads and mountains northerly! –
Yea, to such freshness, fairness, fulness, fineness, freeness,
    Love lures life on.

Show me again the day
    When from the sandy bay
We looked together upon the pestered sea! –
Yea, to such surging, swaying, sighing, swelling, shrinking,
    Love lures life on.

Show me again the hour
    When by the pinnacled tower
We eyed each other and feared futurity! –
Yea, to such bodings, broodings, beatings, blanchings,
            blessings,
    Love lures life on.

Show me again just this:
    The moment of that kiss
Away from the prancing folk, by the strawberry-tree! –
Yea, to such rashness, ratheness, rareness, richness,
    Love lures life on.

Begun November 1898

A Thought in Two Moods

I SAW it – pink and white – revealed
    Upon the white and green;
The white and green was a daisied field,
    The pink and white Ethleen.

And as I looked it seemed in kind
    That difference they had none;
The two fair bodiments combined
    As varied miens of one.

A sense that, in some mouldering year,
    As one they both would lie,
Made me move quickly on to her
    To pass the pale thought by.

She laughed and said: 'Out there, to me,
    You looked so weather-browned,
And brown in clothes, you seemed to be
    Made of the dusty ground!'

Self-Unconscious

ALONG the way
    He walked that day,
Watching shapes that reveries limn,
    And seldom he
    Had eyes to see
The moment that encompassed him.

Bright yellowhammers
    Made mirthful clamours,
And billed long straws with a bustling air,
    And bearing their load
    Flew up the road
That he followed, alone, without interest there.

From bank to ground
And over and round
They sidled along the adjoining hedge;
Sometimes to the gutter
Their yellow flutter
Would dip from the nearest slatestone ledge.

The smooth sea-line
With a metal shine,
And flashes of white, and a sail thereon,
He would also descry
With a half-wrapt eye
Between the projects he mused upon.

Yes, round him were these
Earth's artistries,
But specious plans that came to his call
Did most engage
His pilgrimage,
While himself he did not see at all.

Dead now as sherds
Are the yellow birds,
And all that mattered has passed away;
Yet God, the Elf,
Now shows him that self
As he was, and should have been shown, that day.

O it would have been good
Could he then have stood
At a clear-eyed distance, and conned the whole,
But now such vision
Is mere derision,
Nor soothes his body nor saves his soul.

Not much, some may
Incline to say,
To see therein, had it all been seen.
Nay! he is aware
A thing was there
That loomed with an immortal mien.

Near Bossiney

She Who Saw Not

'DID you see something within the house
That made me call you before the red sunsetting?
Something that all this common scene endows
With a richened impress there can be no forgetting?'

' – I have found nothing to see therein,
O Sage, that should have made you urge me to enter,
Nothing to fire the soul, or the sense to win:
I rate you as a rare misrepresenter!'

' – Go anew, Lady, – in by the right. . . .
Well: why does your face not shine like the face of Moses?'
' – I found no moving thing there save the light
And shadow flung on the wall by the outside roses.'

' – Go yet once more, pray. Look on a seat.'
' – I go. . . . O Sage, it's only a man that sits there
With eyes on the sun. Mute, – average head to feet.'
' – No more?' – 'No more. Just one the place befits there,

'As the rays reach in through the open door,
And he looks at his hand, and the sun glows through his
          fingers,
While he's thinking thoughts whose tenour is no more
To me than the swaying rose-tree shade that lingers.'

No more. And years drew on and on
Till no sun came, dank fogs the house enfolding;
And she saw inside, when the form in the flesh had gone,
As a vision what she had missed when the real beholding.

'We Sat at the Window'

(*Bournemouth, 1875*)

WE sat at the window looking out,
And the rain came down like silken strings
That Swithin's day. Each gutter and spout
Babbled unchecked in the busy way
    Of witless things:
Nothing to read, nothing to see
Seemed in that room for her and me
    On Swithin's day.

We were irked by the scene, by our own selves; yes,
For I did not know, nor did she infer
How much there was to read and guess
By her in me, and to see and crown
    By me in her.
Wasted were two souls in their prime,
And great was the waste, that July time
    When the rain came down.

The Self-Unseeing

HERE is the ancient floor,
Footworn and hollowed and thin,
Here was the former door
Where the dead feet walked in.

She sat here in her chair,
Smiling into the fire;
He who played stood there,
Bowing it higher and higher.

Childlike, I danced in a dream;
Blessings emblazoned that day;
Everything glowed with a gleam;
Yet we were looking away!

'Regret Not Me'

REGRET not me;
Beneath the sunny tree
I lie uncaring, slumbering peacefully.

Swift as the light
I flew my faery flight;
Ecstatically I moved, and feared no night.

I did not know
That heydays fade and go,
But deemed that what was would be always so.

I skipped at morn
Between the yellowing corn,
Thinking it good and glorious to be born.

I ran at eves
Among the piled-up sheaves,
Dreaming, 'I grieve not, therefore nothing grieves.'

Now soon will come
The apple, pear, and plum,
And hinds will sing, and autumn insects hum.

Again you will fare
To cider-makings rare,
And junketings; but I shall not be there.

Yet gaily sing
Until the pewter ring
Those songs we sang when we went gipsying.

And lightly dance
Some triple-timed romance
In coupled figures, and forget mischance;

And mourn not me
Beneath the yellowing tree;
For I shall mind not, slumbering peacefully.

Architectural Masks

I

THERE is a house with ivied walls,
And mullioned windows worn and old,
And the long dwellers in those halls
Have souls that know but sordid calls,
        And daily dote on gold.

II

In blazing brick and plated show
Not far away a 'villa' gleams,
And here a family few may know,
With book and pencil, viol and bow,
        Lead inner lives of dreams.

III

The philosophic passers say,
'See that old mansion mossed and fair,
Poetic souls therein are they:
And O that gaudy box! Away,
        You vulgar people there.'

A Leader of Fashion

NEVER has she known
The way a robin will skip and come,
With an eye half bold, half timorsome,
To the table's edge for a breakfast crumb:

Nor has she seen
A streak of roseate gently drawn
Across the east, that means the dawn,
When, up and out, she foots it on:

Nor has she heard
The rustle of the sparrow's tread
To roost in roof-holes near her head
When dusk bids her, too, seek her bed:

Nor has she watched
Amid a stormy eve's turmoil
The pipkin slowly come to boil,
In readiness for one at toil:

Nor has she hearkened
Through the long night-time, lone and numb,
For sounds of sent-for help to come
Ere the swift-sinking life succumb:

Nor has she ever
Held the loved-lost one on her arm,
Attired with care his straightened form,
As if he were alive and warm:

Yea, never has she
Known, seen, heard, felt, such things as these,
Haps of so many in their degrees
Throughout their count of calvaries!

Overlooking the River Stour

THE swallows flew in the curves of an eight
        Above the river-gleam
        In the wet June's last beam:
Like little crossbows animate
The swallows flew in the curves of an eight
        Above the river-gleam.

Planing up shavings of crystal spray
        A moor-hen darted out
        From the bank thereabout,
And through the stream-shine ripped his way;
Planing up shavings of crystal spray
        A moor-hen darted out.

Closed were the kingcups; and the mead
        Dripped in monotonous green,
        Though the day's morning sheen
Had shown it golden and honeybee'd;
Closed were the kingcups; and the mead
        Dripped in monotonous green.

And never I turned my head, alack,
        While these things met my gaze
        Through the pane's drop-drenched glaze,
To see the more behind my back. . . .
O never I turned, but let, alack,
        These less things hold my gaze!

The Musical Box

        LIFELONG to be
Seemed the fair colour of the time;
That there was standing shadowed near
A spirit who sang to the gentle chime
Of the self-struck notes, I did not hear,
        I did not see.

        Thus did it sing
To the mindless lyre that played indoors
As she came to listen for me without:
'O value what the nonce outpours –
This best of life – that shines about
        Your welcoming!'

        I had slowed along
After the torrid hours were done,
Though still the posts and walls and road
Flung back their sense of the hot-faced sun,
And had walked by Stourside Mill, where broad
        Stream-lilies throng.

And I descried
The dusky house that stood apart,
And her, white-muslined, waiting there
In the porch with high-expectant heart,
While still the thin mechanic air
        Went on inside.

At whiles would flit
Swart bats, whose wings, be-webbed and tanned,
Whirred like the wheels of ancient clocks:
She laughed a hailing as she scanned
Me in the gloom, the tuneful box
        Intoning it.

Lifelong to be
I thought it. That there watched hard by
A spirit who sang to the indoor tune,
'O make the most of what is nigh!'
I did not hear in my dull soul-swoon –
        I did not see.

On Sturminster Foot-Bridge

(Onomatopæic)

RETICULATIONS creep upon the slack stream's face
        When the wind skims irritably past,
The current clucks smartly into each hollow place
That years of flood have scrabbled in the pier's sodden base;
        The floating-lily leaves rot fast.

On a roof stand the swallows ranged in wistful waiting rows,
        Till they arrow off and drop like stones
Among the eyot-withies at whose foot the river flows:
And beneath the roof is she who in the dark world shows
        As a lattice-gleam when midnight moans.

A Two-Years' Idyll

YES; such it was;
Just those two seasons unsought,
Sweeping like summertide wind on our ways;
Moving, as straws,
Hearts quick as ours in those days;
Going like wind, too, and rated as nought
Save as the prelude to plays
Soon to come – larger, life-fraught:
Yes; such it was.

'Nought' it was called,
Even by ourselves – that which springs
Out of the years for all flesh, first or last,
Commonplace, scrawled
Dully on days that go past.
Yet, all the while, it upbore us like wings
Even in hours overcast:
Aye, though this best thing of things,
'Nought' it was called!

What seems it now?
Lost: such beginning was all;
Nothing came after: romance straight forsook
Quickly somehow
Life when we sped from our nook,
Primed for new scenes with designs smart and tall. . . .
– A preface without any book,
A trumpet uplipped, but no call;
That seems it now.

The Interloper

'And I saw the figure and visage of Madness seeking for a home'

THERE are three folk driving in a quaint old chaise,
And the cliff-side track looks green and fair;
I view them talking in quiet glee
As they drop down towards the puffins' lair
    By the roughest of ways;
But another with the three rides on, I see,
    Whom I like not to be there!

No: it's not anybody you think of. Next
A dwelling appears by a slow sweet stream
Where two sit happy and half in the dark:
They read, helped out by a frail-wick'd gleam,
    Some rhythmic text;
But one sits with them whom they don't mark,
    One I'm wishing could not be there.

No: not whom you knew and name. And now
I discern gay diners in a mansion-place,
And the guests dropping wit – pert, prim, or choice,
And the hostess's tender and laughing face,
    And the host's bland brow;
But I cannot help hearing a hollow voice,
    And I'd fain not hear it there.

No: it's not from the stranger you met once. Ah,
Yet a goodlier scene than that succeeds;
People on a lawn – quite a crowd of them. Yes,
And they chatter and ramble as fancy leads;
    And they say, 'Hurrah!'
To a blithe speech made; save one, mirthless,
    Who ought not to be there.

Nay: it's not the pale Form your imagings raise,
That waits on us all at a destined time,
It is not the Fourth Figure the Furnace showed;
O that it were such a shape sublime
        In these latter days!
It is that under which best lives corrode;
        Would, would it could not be there!

'If You Had Known'

            IF you had known
When listening with her to the far-down moan
Of the white-selvaged and empurpled sea,
And rain came on that did not hinder talk,
Or damp your flashing facile gaiety
In turning home, despite the slow wet walk
By crooked ways, and over stiles of stone;
        If you had known

        You would lay roses,
Fifty years thence, on her monument, that discloses
Its graying shape upon the luxuriant green;
Fifty years thence to an hour, by chance led there,
What might have moved you? – yea, had you foreseen
That on the tomb of the selfsame one, gone where
The dawn of every day is as the close is,
        You would lay roses!

    1920

VII Missing Dates

At a Bridal

Nature's Indifference

WHEN you paced forth, to await maternity,
A dream of other offspring held my mind,
Compounded of us twain as Love designed;
Rare forms, that corporate now will never be!

Should I, too, wed as slave to Mode's decree,
And each thus found apart, of false desire,
A stolid line, whom no high aims will fire
As had fired ours could ever have mingled we;

And, grieved that lives so matched should miscompose,
Each mourn the double waste; and question dare
To the Great Dame whence incarnation flows,
Why those high-purposed children never were:
What will she answer? That she does not care
If the race all such sovereign types unknows.

1866

To Louisa in the Lane

MEET me again as at that time
  In the hollow of the lane;
I will not pass as in my prime
  I passed at each day's wane.
    – Ah, I remember!
To do it you will have to see
Anew this sorry scene wherein you have ceased to be!

But I will welcome your aspen form
  As you gaze wondering round
And say with spectral frail alarm,
  'Why am I still here found?
     – Ah, I remember!
It is through him with blitheful brow
Who did not love me then, but loves and draws me now!'

And I shall answer: 'Sweet of eyes,
  Carry me with you, Dear,
To where you donned this spirit-guise;
  It's better there than here!'
     – Till I remember
Such is a deed you cannot do:
Wait must I, till with flung-off flesh I follow you.

Neutral Tones

WE stood by a pond that winter day,
And the sun was white, as though chidden of God,
And a few leaves lay on the starving sod;
    – They had fallen from an ash, and were gray.

Your eyes on me were as eyes that rove
Over tedious riddles of years ago;
And some words played between us to and fro
    On which lost the more by our love.

The smile on your mouth was the deadest thing
Alive enough to have strength to die;
And a grin of bitterness swept thereby
    Like an ominous bird a-wing. . . .

Since then, keen lessons that love deceives,
And wrings with wrong, have shaped to me
Your face, and the God-curst sun, and a tree,
    And a pond edged with grayish leaves.

1867

At Waking

WHEN night was lifting,
And dawn had crept under its shade,
  Amid cold clouds drifting
Dead-white as a corpse outlaid,
      With a sudden scare
      I seemed to behold
      My Love in bare
      Hard lines unfold.

  Yea, in a moment,
An insight that would not die
  Killed her old endowment
Of charm that had capped all nigh,
      Which vanished to none
      Like the gilt of a cloud,
      And showed her but one
      Of the common crowd.

  She seemed but a sample
Of earth's poor average kind,
  Lit up by no ample
Enrichments of mien or mind.
      I covered my eyes
      As to cover the thought,
      And unrecognize
      What the morn had taught.

  O vision appalling
When the one believed-in thing
  Is seen falling, falling,
With all to which hope can cling.
      Off: it is not true;
      For it cannot be
      That the prize I drew
      Is a blank to me!

Weymouth, 1869

'In the Vaulted Way'

IN the vaulted way, where the passage turned
To the shadowy corner that none could see,
You paused for our parting, – plaintively;
Though overnight had come words that burned
My fond frail happiness out of me.

And then I kissed you, – despite my thought
That our spell must end when reflection came
On what you had deemed me, whose one long aim
Had been to serve you; that what I sought
Lay not in a heart that could breathe such blame.

But yet I kissed you; whereon you again
As of old kissed me. Why, why was it so?
Do you cleave to me after that light-tongued blow?
If you scorned me at eventide, how love then?
The thing is dark, Dear. I do not know.

At a Seaside Town in 1869

(*Young Lover's Reverie*)

I WENT and stood outside myself,
        Spelled the dark sky
        And ship-lights nigh,
And grumbling winds that passed thereby.

Then next inside myself I looked,
        And there, above
        All, shone my Love,
That nothing matched the image of.

Beyond myself again I ranged;
        And saw the free
        Life by the sea,
And folk indifferent to me.

O 'twas a charm to draw within
    Thereafter, where
    But she was; care
For one thing only, her hid there!

But so it chanced, without myself
    I had to look,
    And then I took
More heed of what I had long forsook:

The boats, the sands, the esplanade,
    The laughing crowd;
    Light-hearted, loud
Greetings from some not ill-endowed;

The evening sunlit cliffs, the talk,
    Hailings and halts,
    The keen sea-salts,
The band, the Morgenblätter Waltz.

Still, when at night I drew inside
    Forward she came,
    Sad, but the same
As when I first had known her name.

Then rose a time when, as by force,
    Outwardly wooed
    By contacts crude,
Her image in abeyance stood. . . .

At last I said: This outside life
    Shall not endure;
    I'll seek the pure
Thought-world, and bask in her allure.

Myself again I crept within,
    Scanned with keen care
    The temple where
She'd shone, but could not find her there.

I sought and sought. But O her soul
    Has not since thrown
    Upon my own
One beam! Yea, she is gone, is gone.

From an old note

The Contretemps

A FORWARD rush by the lamp in the gloom,
    And we clasped, and almost kissed;
But she was not the woman whom
I had promised to meet in the thawing brume
On that harbour-bridge; nor was I he of her tryst.

So loosening from me swift she said:
    'O why, why feign to be
The one I had meant! – to whom I have sped
To fly with, being so sorrily wed!'
– 'Twas thus and thus that she upbraided me.

My assignation had struck upon
    Some others' like it, I found.
And her lover rose on the night anon;
And then her husband entered on
The lamplit, snowflaked, sloppiness around.

'Take her and welcome, man!' he cried:
    'I wash my hands of her.
I'll find me twice as good a bride!'
– All this to me, whom he had eyed,
Plainly, as his wife's planned deliverer.

And next the lover: 'Little I knew,
    Madam, you had a third!
Kissing here in my very view!'
– Husband and lover then withdrew.
I let them; and I told them not they erred.

Why not? Well, there faced she and I –
    Two strangers who'd kissed, or near,
Chancewise. To see stand weeping by
A woman once embraced, will try
The tension of a man the most austere.

So it began; and I was young,
    She pretty, by the lamp,
As flakes came waltzing down among
The waves of her clinging hair, that hung
Heavily on her temples, dark and damp.

And there alone still stood we two;
    She one cast off for me,
Or so it seemed: while night ondrew,
Forcing a parley what should do
We twain hearts caught in one catastrophe.

In stranded souls a common strait
    Wakes latencies unknown,
Whose impulse may precipitate
A life-long leap. The hour was late,
And there was the Jersey boat with its funnel agroan.

'Is wary walking worth much pother?'
    It grunted, as still it stayed.
'One pairing is as good as another
Where all is venture! Take each other,
And scrap the oaths that you have aforetime made.' . . .

– Of the four involved there walks but one
    On earth at this late day.
And what of the chapter so begun?
In that odd complex what was done?
Well; happiness comes in full to none:
Let peace lie on lulled lips: I will not say.

Weymouth

The Photograph

THE flame crept up the portrait line by line
As it lay on the coals in the silence of night's profound,
    And over the arm's incline,
And along the marge of the silkwork superfine,
And gnawed at the delicate bosom's defenceless round.

Then I vented a cry of hurt, and averted my eyes;
The spectacle was one that I could not bear,
    To my deep and sad surprise;
But, compelled to heed, I again looked furtivewise
Till the flame had eaten her breasts, and mouth, and hair.

'Thank God, she is out of it now!' I said at last,
In a great relief of heart when the thing was done
    That had set my soul aghast,
And nothing was left of the picture unsheathed from the past
But the ashen ghost of the card it had figured on.

She was a woman long hid amid packs of years,
She might have been living or dead; she was lost to my sight,
    And the deed that had nigh drawn tears
Was done in a casual clearance of life's arrears;
But I felt as if I had put her to death that night! . . .

                .   .   .

– Well; she knew nothing thereof did she survive,
And suffered nothing if numbered among the dead;
    Yet – yet – if on earth alive
Did she feel a smart, and with vague strange anguish strive?
If in heaven, did she smile at me sadly and shake her head?

Thoughts of Phena

At News of Her Death

NOT a line of her writing have I,
    Not a thread of her hair,
No mark of her late time as dame in her dwelling, whereby
    I may picture her there;
    And in vain do I urge my unsight
    To conceive my lost prize
At her close, whom I knew when her dreams were
   upbrimming with light,
    And with laughter her eyes.

   What scenes spread around her last days,
    Sad, shining, or dim?
Did her gifts and compassions enray and enarch her sweet
   ways
    With an aureate nimb?
   Or did life-light decline from her years,
    And mischances control
Her full day-star; unease, or regret, or forebodings, or fears
    Disennoble her soul?

   Thus I do but the phantom retain
    Of the maiden of yore
As my relic; yet haply the best of her – fined in my brain
    It may be the more
   That no line of her writing have I,
    Nor a thread of her hair,
No mark of her late time as dame in her dwelling, whereby
    I may picture her there.

March 1890

The Recalcitrants

LET us off and search, and find a place
Where yours and mine can be natural lives,
Where no one comes who dissects and dives
And proclaims that ours is a curious case,
Which its touch of romance can scarcely grace.

You would think it strange at first, but then
.Everything has been strange in its time.
When some one said on a day of the prime
He would bow to no brazen god again
He doubtless dazed the mass of men.

None will see in us a pair whose claims
To righteous judgment we care not making;
Who have doubted if breath be worth the taking,
And have no respect for the current fames
Whence the savour has flown while abide the names.

We have found us already shunned, disdained,
And for re-acceptance have not once striven;
Whatever offence our course has given
The brunt thereof we have long sustained.
Well, let us away, scorned, unexplained.

The Mound

FOR a moment pause: –
    Just here it was;
And through the thin thorn hedge, by the rays of the
        moon,
I can see the tree in the field, and beside it the mound –
Now sheeted with snow – whereon we sat that June
    When it was green and round,
And she crazed my mind by what she coolly told –
    The history of her undoing,
(As I saw it), but she called 'comradeship',
    That bred in her no rueing:

And saying she'd not be bound
For life to one man, young, ripe-yeared, or old,
Left me – an innocent simpleton to her viewing;
For, though my accompt of years outscored her own,
    Hers had more hotly flown. . . .
We never met again by this green mound,
To press as once so often lip on lip,
        And palter, and pause: –
        Yes; here it was!

On the Departure Platform

WE kissed at the barrier; and passing through
She left me, and moment by moment got
Smaller and smaller, until to my view
        She was but a spot;

A wee white spot of muslin fluff
That down the diminishing platform bore
Through hustling crowds of gentle and rough
        To the carriage door.

Under the lamplight's fitful glowers,
Behind dark groups from far and near,
Whose interests were apart from ours,
        She would disappear,

Then show again, till I ceased to see
That flexible form, that nebulous white;
And she who was more than my life to me
        Had vanished quite. . . .

We have penned new plans since that fair fond day,
And in season she will appear again –
Perhaps in the same soft white array –
        But never as then!

– 'And why, young man, must eternally fly
A joy you'll repeat, if you love her well?'
– O friend, nought happens twice thus; why,
        I cannot tell!

Alike and Unlike

(Great-Orme's Head)

WE watched the selfsame scene on that long drive,
Saw the magnificent purples, as one eye,
Of those near mountains; saw the storm arrive;
Laid up the sight in memory, you and I,
As if for joint recallings by and by.

But our eye-records, like in hue and line,
Had superimposed on them, that very day,
Gravings on your side deep, but slight on mine! –
Tending to sever us thenceforth alway;
Mine commonplace; yours tragic, gruesome, gray.

The Division

RAIN on the windows, creaking doors,
　　With blasts that besom the green,
And I am here, and you are there,
　　And a hundred miles between!

O were it but the weather, Dear,
　　O were it but the miles
That summed up all our severance,
　　There might be room for smiles.

But that thwart thing betwixt us twain,
　　Which nothing cleaves or clears,
Is more than distance, Dear, or rain,
　　And longer than the years!

1893

A Thunderstorm in Town

(*A Reminiscence: 1893*)

SHE wore a new 'terra-cotta' dress,
And we stayed, because of the pelting storm,
Within the hansom's dry recess,
Though the horse had stopped; yea, motionless
    We sat on, snug and warm.

Then the downpour ceased, to my sharp sad pain,
And the glass that had screened our forms before
Flew up, and out she sprang to her door:
I should have kissed her if the rain
    Had lasted a minute more.

At an Inn

WHEN we as strangers sought
    Their catering care,
Veiled smiles bespoke their thought
    Of what we were.
They warmed as they opined
    Us more than friends –
That we had all resigned
    For love's dear ends.

And that swift sympathy
    With living love
Which quicks the world – maybe
    The spheres above,
Made them our ministers,
    Moved them to say,
'Ah, God, that bliss like theirs
    Would flush our day!'

And we were left alone
  As Love's own pair;
Yet never the love-light shone
  Between us there!
But that which chilled the breath
  Of afternoon,
And palsied unto death
  The pane-fly's tune.

The kiss their zeal foretold,
  And now deemed come,
Came not: within his hold
  Love lingered numb.
Why cast he on our port
  A bloom not ours?
Why shaped us for his sport
  In after-hours?

As we seemed we were not
  That day afar,
And now we seem not what
  We aching are.
O severing sea and land,
  O laws of men,
Ere death, once let us stand
  As we stood then!

A Beauty's Soliloquy during Her Honeymoon

Too late, too late! I did not know my fairness
  Would catch the world's keen eyes so!
How the men look at me! My radiant rareness
  I deemed not they would prize so!

That I was a peach for any man's possession
  Why did not some one say
Before I leased myself in an hour's obsession
  To this dull mate for aye!

His days are mine. I am one who cannot steal her
    Ahead of his plodding pace:
As he is, so am I. One doomed to feel her
    A wasted form and face!

I was so blind! It did sometimes just strike me
    All girls were not as I,
But, dwelling much alone, how few were like me
    I could not well descry;

Till, at this Grand Hotel, all looks bend on me
    In homage as I pass
To take my seat at breakfast, dinner, – con me
    As poorly spoused, alas!

I was too young. I dwelt too much on duty:
    If I had guessed my powers
Where might have sailed this cargo of choice beauty
    In its unanchored hours!

Well, husband, poor plain man; I've lost life's battle! –
    Come – let them look at me.
O damn, don't show in your looks that I'm your chattel
    Quite so emphatically!

In a London Hotel, 1892

Faintheart in a Railway Train

At nine in the morning there passed a church,
At ten there passed me by the sea,
At twelve a town of smoke and smirch,
At two a forest of oak and birch,
    And then, on a platform, she:

A radiant stranger, who saw not me.
I said, 'Get out to her do I dare?'
But I kept my seat in my search for a plea,
And the wheels moved on. O could it but be
    That I had alighted there!

A Broken Appointment

You did not come,
And marching Time drew on, and wore me numb. –
Yet less for loss of your dear presence there
Than that I thus found lacking in your make
That high compassion which can overbear
Reluctance for pure lovingkindness' sake
Grieved I, when, as the hope-hour stroked its sum,
You did not come.

You love not me,
And love alone can lend you loyalty;
– I know and knew it. But, unto the store
Of human deeds divine in all but name,
Was it not worth a little hour or more
To add yet this: Once you, a woman, came
To soothe a time-torn man; even though it be
You love not me?

'Had You Wept'

Had you wept; had you but neared me with a hazed
uncertain ray,
Dewy as the face of the dawn, in your large and luminous
eye,
Then would have come back all the joys the tidings had slain
that day,
And a new beginning, a fresh fair heaven, have smoothed
the things awry.
But you were less feebly human, and no passionate need for
clinging
Possessed your soul to overthrow reserve when I came
near;
Ay, though you suffer as much as I from storms the hours are
bringing
Upon your heart and mine, I never see you shed a tear.

The deep strong woman is weakest, the weak one is the
    strong;
The weapon of all weapons best for winning, you have not
    used;
Have you never been able, or would you not, through the
    evil times and long?
Has not the gift been given you, or such gift have you
    refused?
When I bade me not absolve you on that evening or the
    morrow,
Why did you not make war on me with those who weep like
    rain?
You felt too much, so gained no balm for all your torrid
    sorrow,
And hence our deep division, and our dark undying pain.

After the Visit

(To F.E.D.)

COME again to the place
Where your presence was as a leaf that skims
Down a drouthy way whose ascent bedims
    The bloom on the farer's face.

Come again, with the feet
That were light on the green as a thistledown ball,
And those mute ministrations to one and to all
    Beyond a man's saying sweet.

Until then the faint scent
Of the bordering flowers swam unheeded away,
And I marked not the charm in the changes of day
    As the cloud-colours came and went.

Through the dark corridors
Your walk was so soundless I did not know
Your form from a phantom's of long ago
    Said to pass on the ancient floors,

Till you drew from the shade,
And I saw the large luminous living eyes
Regard me in fixed inquiring-wise
        As those of a soul that weighed,

Scarce consciously,
The eternal question of what Life was,
And why we were there, and by whose strange laws
        That which mattered most could not be.

To Lizbie Browne

I

DEAR Lizbie Browne,
Where are you now?
In sun, in rain? –
Or is your brow
Past joy, past pain,
Dear Lizbie Browne?

II

Sweet Lizbie Browne,
How you could smile,
How you could sing! –
How archly wile
In glance-giving,
Sweet Lizbie Browne!

III

And, Lizbie Browne,
Who else had hair
Bay-red as yours,
Or flesh so fair
Bred out of doors,
Sweet Lizbie Browne?

IV

When, Lizbie Browne,
You had just begun
To be endeared
By stealth to one,
You disappeared
My Lizbie Browne!

V

Ay, Lizbie Browne,
So swift your life,
And mine so slow,
You were a wife
Ere I could show
Love, Lizbie Browne.

VI

Still, Lizbie Browne,
You won, they said,
The best of men
When you were wed. . . .
Where went you then,
O Lizbie Browne?

VII

Dear Lizbie Browne,
I should have thought,
'Girls ripen fast,'
And coaxed and caught
You ere you passed,
Dear Lizbie Browne!

VIII

But, Lizbie Browne,
I let you slip;
Shaped not a sign;
Touched never your lip
With lip of mine,
Lost Lizbie Browne!

IX

So, Lizbie Browne,
When on a day
Men speak of me
As not, you'll say,
'And who was he?' –
Yes, Lizbie Browne!

A Countenance

HER laugh was not in the middle of her face quite,
    As a gay laugh springs,
It was plain she was anxious about some things
    I could not trace quite.
Her curls were like fir-cones – piled up, brown –
    Or rather like tight-tied sheaves:
It seemed they could never be taken down. . . .

And her lips were too full, some might say:
I did not think so. Anyway,
The shadow her lower one would cast
Was green in hue whenever she passed
    Bright sun on midsummer leaves.
Alas, I knew not much of her,
And lost all sight and touch of her!

If otherwise, should I have minded
The shy laugh not in the middle of her mouth quite,
And would my kisses have died of drouth quite
    As love became unblinded?

1884

At Rushy-Pond

ON the frigid face of the heath-hemmed pond
    There shaped the half-grown moon:
Winged whiffs from the north with a husky croon
    Blew over and beyond.

And the wind flapped the moon in its float on the pool,
    And stretched it to oval form;
Then corkscrewed it like a wriggling worm;
    Then wanned it weariful.

And I cared not for conning the sky above
    Where hung the substant thing,
For my thought was earthward sojourning
    On the scene I had vision of.

Since there it was once, in a secret year,
    I had called a woman to me
From across this water, ardently –
    And practised to keep her near;

Till the last weak love-words had been said,
    And ended was her time,
And blurred the bloomage of her prime,
    And white the earlier red.

And the troubled orb in the pond's sad shine
    Was her very wraith, as scanned
When she withdrew thence, mirrored, and
    Her days dropped out of mine.

To a Motherless Child

AH, child, thou art but half thy darling mother's;
    Hers couldst thou wholly be,
My light in thee would outglow all in others;
    She would relive to me.

But niggard Nature's trick of birth
  Bars, lest she overjoy,
Renewal of the loved on earth
  Save with alloy.

The Dame has no regard, alas, my maiden,
  For love and loss like mine –
No sympathy with mindsight memory-laden;
  Only with fickle eyne.
To her mechanic artistry
  My dreams are all unknown,
And why I wish that thou couldst be
  But One's alone!

Concerning Agnes

I AM stopped from hoping what I have hoped before –
  Yes, many a time! –
To dance with that fair woman yet once more
  As in the prime
Of August, when the wide-faced moon looked through
The boughs at the faery lamps of the Larmer Avenue.

I could not, though I should wish, have over again
  That old romance,
And sit apart in the shade as we sat then
  After the dance
The while I held her hand, and, to the booms
Of contrabassos, feet still pulsed from the distant rooms.

I could not. And you do not ask me why.
  Hence you infer
That what may chance to the fairest under the sky
  Has chanced to her.
Yes. She lies white, straight, features marble-keen,
Unapproachable, mute, in a nook I have never seen.

There she may rest like some vague goddess, shaped
     As out of snow;
Say Aphrodite sleeping; or bedraped
     Like Kalupso;
Or Amphitrite stretched on the Mid-sea swell,
Or one of the Nine grown stiff from thought. I cannot tell!

Louie

I AM forgetting Louie the buoyant;
   Why not raise her phantom, too,
     Here in daylight
     With the elect one's?
She will never thrust the foremost figure out of view!

Mid this heat, in gauzy muslin
   See I Louie's life-lit brow
     Here in daylight
     By the elect one's. –
Long two strangers they and far apart; such neighbours now!

July 1913

In Death Divided

I

I SHALL rot here, with those whom in their day
     You never knew,
And alien ones who, ere they chilled to clay,
     Met not my view,
Will in your distant grave-place ever neighbour you.

II

No shade of pinnacle or tree or tower,
    While earth endures,
Will fall on my mound and within the hour
    Steal on to yours;
One robin never haunt our two green covertures.

III

Some organ may resound on Sunday noons
    By where you lie,
Some other thrill the panes with other tunes
    Where moulder I;
No selfsame chords compose our common lullaby.

IV

The simply-cut memorial at my head
    Perhaps may take
A rustic form, and that above your bed
    A stately make;
No linking symbol show thereon for our tale's sake.

V

And in the monotonous moils of strained, hard-run
    Humanity,
The eternal tie which binds us twain in one
    No eye will see
Stretching across the miles that sever you from me.

189–

The Five Students

THE sparrow dips in his wheel-rut bath,
    The sun grows passionate-eyed,
And boils the dew to smoke by the paddock-path;
    As strenuously we stride, –
Five of us; dark He, fair He, dark She, fair She, I,
    All beating by.

The air is shaken, the high-road hot,
    Shadowless swoons the day,
The greens are sobered and cattle at rest; but not
    We on our urgent way, –
Four of us; fair She, dark She, fair He, I, are there,
    But one – elsewhere.

Autumn moulds the hard fruit mellow,
    And forward still we press
Through moors, briar-meshed plantations, clay-pits
    yellow,
    As in the spring hours – yes,
Three of us; fair He, fair She, I, as heretofore,
    But – fallen one more.

The leaf drops: earthworms draw it in
    At night-time noiselessly,
The fingers of birch and beech are skeleton-thin,
    And yet on the beat are we, –
Two of us; fair She, I. But no more left to go
    The track we know.

Icicles tag the church-aisle leads,
    The flag-rope gibbers hoarse,
The home-bound foot-folk wrap their snow-flaked heads,
    Yet I still stalk the course –
One of us. . . . Dark and fair He, dark and fair She, gone:
    The rest – anon.

Nobody Comes

TREE-LEAVES labour up and down,
    And through them the fainting light
    Succumbs to the crawl of night.
Outside in the road the telegraph wire
    To the town from the darkening land
Intones to travellers like a spectral lyre
    Swept by a spectral hand.

A car comes up, with lamps full-glare,
That flash upon a tree:
It has nothing to do with me,
And whangs along in a world of its own,
Leaving a blacker air;
And mute by the gate I stand again alone,
And nobody pulls up there.

9 October 1924

VIII Your Great Going

On the Esplanade

Midsummer: 10 p.m.

THE broad bald moon edged up where the sea was wide,
    Mild, mellow-faced;
Beneath, a tumbling twinkle of shines, like dyed,
    A trackway traced
To the shore, as of petals fallen from a rose to waste,
    In its overblow,
And fluttering afloat on inward heaves of the tide: –
All this, so plain; yet the rest I did not know.

The horizon gets lost in a mist new-wrought by the night:
    The lamps of the Bay
That reach from behind me round to the left and right
    On the sea-wall way
For a constant mile of curve, make a long display
    As a pearl-strung row,
Under which in the waves they bore their gimlets of light: –
All this was plain; but there was a thing not so.

Inside a window, open, with undrawn blind,
    There plays and sings
A lady unseen a melody undefined:
    And where the moon flings
Its shimmer a vessel crosses, whereon to the strings
    Plucked sweetly and low
Of a harp, they dance. Yea, such did I mark. That, behind,
My Fate's masked face crept near me I did not know!

The Wind's Prophecy

I TRAVEL on by barren farms,
And gulls glint out like silver flecks
Against a cloud that speaks of wrecks,
And bellies down with black alarms.
I say: 'Thus from my lady's arms
I go; those arms I love the best!'
The wind replies from dip and rise,
'Nay; toward her arms thou journeyest.'

A distant verge morosely gray
Appears, while clots of flying foam
Break from its muddy monochrome,
And a light blinks up far away.
I sigh: 'My eyes now as all day
Behold her ebon loops of hair!'
Like bursting bonds the wind responds,
'Nay, wait for tresses flashing fair!'

From tides the lofty coastlands screen
Come smitings like the slam of doors,
Or hammerings on hollow floors,
As the swell cleaves through caves unseen.
Say I: 'Though broad this wild terrene,
Her city home is matched of none!'
From the hoarse skies the wind replies:
'Thou shouldst have said her sea-bord one.'

The all-prevailing clouds exclude
The one quick timorous transient star;
The waves outside where breakers are
Huzza like a mad multitude.
'Where the sun ups it, mist-imbued,'
I cry, 'there reigns the star for me!'
The wind outshrieks from points and peaks:
'Here, westward, where it downs, mean ye!'

Yonder the headland, vulturine,
Snores like old Skrymer in his sleep,
And every chasm and every steep
Blackens as wakes each pharos-shine.
'I roam, but one is safely mine,'
I say. 'God grant she stay my own!'
Low laughs the wind as if it grinned:
'Thy Love is one thou'st not yet known.'

Rewritten from an old copy

'When I Set Out for Lyonnesse'

(*1870*)

WHEN I set out for Lyonnesse,
    A hundred miles away,
    The rime was on the spray,
And starlight lit my lonesomeness
When I set out for Lyonnesse
    A hundred miles away.

What would bechance at Lyonnesse
    While I should sojourn there
    No prophet durst declare,
Nor did the wisest wizard guess
What would bechance at Lyonnesse
    While I should sojourn there.

When I came back from Lyonnesse
    With magic in my eyes,
    All marked with mute surmise
My radiance rare and fathomless,
When I came back from Lyonnesse
    With magic in my eyes!

A Man Was Drawing Near to Me

ON that gray night of mournful drone,
Apart from aught to hear, to see,
I dreamt not that from shires unknown
    In gloom, alone,
      By Halworthy,
A man was drawing near to me.

I'd no concern at anything,
No sense of coming pull-heart play;
Yet, under the silent outspreading
    Of even's wing
      Where Otterham lay,
A man was riding up my way.

I though of nobody – not of one,
But only of trifles – legends, ghosts –
Though, on the moorland dim and dun
    That travellers shun
      About these coasts,
The man had passed Tresparret Posts.

There was no light at all inland,
Only the seaward pharos-fire,
Nothing to let me understand
    That hard at hand
      By Hennett Byre
The man was getting nigh and nigher.

There was a rumble at the door,
A draught disturbed the drapery,
And but a minute passed before,
    With gaze that bore
      My destiny,
The man revealed himself to me.

At the Word 'Farewell'

SHE looked like a bird from a cloud
 On the clammy lawn,
Moving alone, bare-browed
 In the dim of dawn.
The candles alight in the room
 For my parting meal
Made all things withoutdoors loom
 Strange, ghostly, unreal.

The hour itself was a ghost,
 And it seemed to me then
As of chances the chance furthermost
 I should see her again.
I beheld not where all was so fleet
 That a Plan of the past
Which had ruled us from birthtime to meet
 Was in working at last:

No prelude did I there perceive
 To a drama at all,
Or foreshadow what fortune might weave
 From beginnings so small;
But I rose as if quicked by a spur
 I was bound to obey,
And stepped through the casement to her
 Still alone in the gray.

'I am leaving you. . . . Farewell!' I said,
 As I followed her on
By an alley bare boughs overspread;
 'I soon must be gone!'
Even then the scale might have been turned
 Against love by a feather,
– But crimson one cheek of hers burned
 When we came in together.

First Sight of Her and After

A DAY is drawing to its fall
    I had not dreamed to see;
The first of many to enthrall
    My spirit, will it be?
Or is this eve the end of all
    Such new delight for me?

I journey home: the pattern grows
    Of moonshades on the way:
'Soon the first quarter, I suppose,'
    Sky-glancing travellers say;
I realize that it, for those,
    Has been a common day.

Ditty

(E.L.G.)

BENEATH a knap where flown
    Nestlings play,
Within walls of weathered stone,
    Far away
From the files of formal houses,
By the bough the firstling browses,
Lives a Sweet: no merchants meet,
No man barters, no man sells
    Where she dwells.

Upon that fabric fair
    'Here is she!'
Seems written everywhere
    Unto me.
But to friends and nodding neighbours,
Fellow-wights in lot and labours,
Who descry the times as I,
No such lucid legend tells
    Where she dwells.

Should I lapse to what I was
    Ere we met;
(Such will not be, but because
    Some forget
Let me feign it) – none would notice
That where she I know by rote is
Spread a strange and withering change,
Like a drying of the wells
    Where she dwells.

To feel I might have kissed –
    Loved as true –
Otherwhere, nor Mine have missed
    My life through,
Had I never wandered near her,
Is a smart severe – severer
In the thought that she is nought,
Even as I, beyond the dells
    Where she dwells.

And Devotion droops her glance
    To recall
What bond-servants of Chance
    We are all.
I but found her in that, going
On my errant path unknowing,
I did not out-skirt the spot
That no spot on earth excels,
    – Where she dwells!

1870

Fetching Her

AN hour before the dawn,
    My friend,
You lit your waiting bedside-lamp,
   Your breakfast-fire anon,
And outing into the dark and damp
   You saddled, and set on.

Thuswise, before the day,
My friend,
You sought her on her surfy shore,
To fetch her thence away
Unto your own new-builded door
For a staunch lifelong stay.

You said: 'It seems to be,
My friend,
That I were bringing to my place
The pure brine breeze, the sea,
The mews – all her old sky and space,
In bringing her with me!'

– But time is prompt to expugn,
My friend,
Such magic-minted conjurings:
The brought breeze fainted soon,
And then the sense of seamews' wings,
And the shore's sibilant tune.

So, it had been more due,
My friend,
Perhaps, had you not pulled this flower
From the craggy nook it knew,
And set it in an alien bower;
But left it where it grew!

A Second Attempt

THIRTY years after
I began again
An old-time passion:
And it seemed as fresh as when
The first day ventured on:
When mutely I would waft her
In Love's past fashion
Dreams much dwelt upon,
Dreams I wished she knew.

I went the course through,
From Love's fresh-found sensation –
Remembered still so well –
To worn words charged anew,
That left no more to tell:
Thence to hot hopes and fears,
And thence to consummation,
And thence to sober years,
Markless, and mellow-hued.

Firm the whole fabric stood,
Or seemed to stand, and sound
As it had stood before.
But nothing backward climbs,
And when I looked around
As at the former times,
There was Life – pale and hoar;
And slow it said to me,
'Twice-over cannot be!'

Lost Love

I PLAY my sweet old airs –
   The airs he knew
    When our love was true –
    But he does not balk
    His determined walk,
And passes up the stairs.

I sing my songs once more,
    And presently hear
    His footstep near
    As if it would stay;
    But he goes his way,
And shuts a distant door.

So I wait for another morn,
    And another night
    In this soul-sick blight;

And I wonder much
As I sit, why such
A woman as I was born!

Lonely Days

LONELY her fate was,
Environed from sight
In the house where the gate was
Past finding at night.
None there to share it,
No one to tell:
Long she'd to bear it,
And bore it well.

Elsewhere just so she
Spent many a day;
Wishing to go she
Continued to stay.
And people without
Basked warm in the air,
But none sought her out,
Or knew she was there.
Even birthdays were passed so,
Sunny and shady:
Years did it last so
For this sad lady.
Never declaring it,
No one to tell,
Still she kept bearing it –
Bore it well.

The days grew chillier,
And then she went
To a city, familiar
In years forespent,
When she walked gaily
Far to and fro,
But now, moving fraily,
Could nowhere go.

The cheerful colour
Of houses she'd known
Had died to a duller
And dingier tone.
Streets were now noisy
Where once had rolled
A few quiet coaches,
Or citizens strolled.
Through the party-wall
Of the memoried spot
They danced at a ball
Who recalled her not.
Tramlines lay crossing
Once gravelled slopes,
Metal rods clanked,
And electric ropes.
So she endured it all,
Thin, thinner wrought,
Until time cured it all,
And she knew nought.

Versified from a Diary

Under the Waterfall

'WHENEVER I plunge my arm, like this,
In a basin of water, I never miss
The sweet sharp sense of a fugitive day
Fetched back from its thickening shroud of gray.
        Hence the only prime
        And real love-rhyme
        That I know by heart,
        And that leaves no smart,
Is the purl of a little valley fall
About three spans wide and two spans tall
Over a table of solid rock,
And into a scoop of the self-same block;
The purl of a runlet that never ceases
In stir of kingdoms, in wars, in peaces;

With a hollow boiling voice it speaks
And has spoken since hills were turfless peaks.'

'And why gives this the only prime
Idea to you of a real love-rhyme?
And why does plunging your arm in a bowl
Full of spring water, bring throbs to your soul?'

'Well, under the fall, in a crease of the stone,
Though where precisely none ever has known,
Jammed darkly, nothing to show how prized,
And by now with its smoothness opalized,
       Is a drinking-glass:
       For, down that pass
       My lover and I
       Walked under a sky
Of blue with a leaf-wove awning of green,
In the burn of August, to paint the scene,
And we placed our basket of fruit and wine
By the runlet's rim, where we sat to dine;
And when we had drunk from the glass together,
Arched by the oak-copse from the weather,
I held the vessel to rinse in the fall,
Where it slipped, and sank, and was past recall,
Though we stooped and plumbed the little abyss
With long bared arms. There the glass still is.
And, as said, if I thrust my arm below
Cold water in basin or bowl, a throe
From the past awakens a sense of that time,
And the glass we used, and the cascade's rhyme.
The basin seems the pool, and its edge
The hard smooth face of the brook-side ledge,
And the leafy pattern of china-ware
The hanging plants that were bathing there.

'By night, by day, when it shines or lours,
There lies intact that chalice of ours,
And its presence adds to the rhyme of love
Persistently sung by the fall above.
No lip has touched it since his and mine
In turns therefrom sipped lovers' wine.'

'She Opened the Door'

SHE opened the door of the West to me,
    With its loud sea-lashings,
    And cliff-side clashings
Of waters rife with revelry.

She opened the door of Romance to me,
    The door from a cell
    I had known too well,
Too long, till then, and was fain to flee.

She opened the door of a Love to me,
    That passed the wry
    World-welters by
As far as the arching blue the lea.

She opens the door of the Past to me,
    Its magic lights,
    Its heavenly heights,
When forward little is to see!

1913

The Going

WHY did you give no hint that night
That quickly after the morrow's dawn,
And calmly, as if indifferent quite,
You would close your term here, up and be gone
    Where I could not follow
    With wing of swallow
To gain one glimpse of you ever anon!

    Never to bid good-bye,
    Or lip me the softest call,
Or utter a wish for a word, while I
Saw morning harden upon the wall,

Unmoved, unknowing
That your great going
Had place that moment, and altered all.

Why do you make me leave the house
And think for a breath it is you I see
At the end of the alley of bending boughs
Where so often at dusk you used to be;
Till in darkening dankness
The yawning blankness
Of the perspective sickens me!

You were she who abode
By those red-veined rocks far West,
You were the swan-necked one who rode
Along the beetling Beeny Crest,
And, reining nigh me,
Would muse and eye me,
While Life unrolled us its very best.

Why, then, latterly did we not speak,
Did we not think of those days long dead,
And ere your vanishing strive to seek
That time's renewal? We might have said,
'In this bright spring weather
We'll visit together
Those places that once we visited.'

Well, well! All's past amend,
Unchangeable. It must go.
I seem but a dead man held on end
To sink down soon. . . . O you could not know
That such swift fleeing
No soul foreseeing –
Not even I – would undo me so!

December 1912

Your Last Drive

HERE by the moorway you returned,
And saw the borough lights ahead
That lit your face – all undiscerned
To be in a week the face of the dead,
And you told of the charm of that haloed view
That never again would beam on you.

And on your left you passed the spot
Where eight days later you were to lie,
And be spoken of as one who was not;
Beholding it with a heedless eye
As alien from you, though under its tree
You soon would halt everlastingly.

I drove not with you. . . . Yet had I sat
At your side that eve I should not have seen
That the countenance I was glancing at
Had a last-time look in the flickering sheen,
Nor have read the writing upon your face,
'I go hence soon to my resting-place;

'You may miss me then. But I shall not know
How many times you visit me there,
Or what your thoughts are, or if you go
There never at all. And I shall not care.
Should you censure me I shall take no heed,
And even your praises no more shall need.'

True: never you'll know. And you will not mind.
But shall I then slight you because of such?
Dear ghost, in the past did you ever find
The thought 'What profit,' move me much?
Yet abides the fact, indeed, the same, –
You are past love, praise, indifference, blame.

December 1912

The Walk

YOU did not walk with me
Of late to the hill-top tree
    By the gated ways,
    As in earlier days;
    You were weak and lame,
    So you never came,
And I went alone, and I did not mind,
Not thinking of you as left behind.

    I walked up there to-day
    Just in the former way;
        Surveyed around
        The familiar ground
        By myself again:
        What difference, then?
Only that underlying sense
Of the look of a room on returning thence.

Rain on a Grave

CLOUDS spout upon her
    Their waters amain
    In ruthless disdain, –
Her who but lately
    Had shivered with pain
As at touch of dishonour
If there had lit on her
So coldly, so straightly
    Such arrows of rain:

One who to shelter
    Her delicate head
Would quicken and quicken
    Each tentative tread
If drops chanced to pelt her
    That summertime spills
    In dust-paven rills

When thunder-clouds thicken
  And birds close their bills.

Would that I lay there
  And she were housed here!
Or better, together
Were folded away there
Exposed to one weather
We both, – who would stray there
When sunny the day there,
  Or evening was clear
  At the prime of the year.

Soon will be growing
  Green blades from her mound,
And daisies be showing
  Like stars on the ground,
Till she form part of them –
Ay – the sweet heart of them,
Loved beyond measure
With a child's pleasure
  All her life's round.

31 Jan. 1913

'I Found Her Out There'

I FOUND her out there
On a slope few see,
That falls westwardly
To the salt-edged air,
Where the ocean breaks
On the purple strand,
And the hurricane shakes
The solid land.

I brought her here,
And have laid her to rest
In a noiseless nest
No sea beats near.

She will never be stirred
In her loamy cell
By the waves long heard
And loved so well.

So she does not sleep
By those haunted heights
The Atlantic smites
And the blind gales sweep,
Whence she often would gaze
At Dundagel's famed head,
While the dipping blaze
Dyed her face fire-red;

And would sigh at the tale
Of sunk Lyonnesse,
As a wind-tugged tress
Flapped her cheek like a flail;
Or listen at whiles
With a thought-bound brow
To the murmuring miles
She is far from now.

Yet her shade, maybe,
Will creep underground
Till it catch the sound
Of that western sea
As it swells and sobs
Where she once domiciled,
And joys in its throbs
With the heart of a child.

Without Ceremony

IT was your way, my dear,
To vanish without a word
When callers, friends, or kin
Had left, and I hastened in
To rejoin you, as I inferred.

And when you'd a mind to career
Off anywhere – say to town –
You were all on a sudden gone
Before I had thought thereon,
Or noticed your trunks were down.

So, now that you disappear
For ever in that swift style,
Your meaning seems to me
Just as it used to be:
'Good-bye is not worth while!'

The Haunter

HE does not think that I haunt here nightly:
    How shall I let him know
That whither his fancy sets him wandering
    I, too, alertly go? –
Hover and hover a few feet from him
    Just as I used to do,
But cannot answer the words he lifts me –
    Only listen thereto!

When I could answer he did not say them:
    When I could let him know
How I would like to join in his journeys
    Seldom he wished to go.
Now that he goes and wants me with him
    More than he used to do,
Never he sees my faithful phantom
    Though he speaks thereto.

Yes, I companion him to places
    Only dreamers know,
Where the shy hares print long paces,
    Where the night rooks go;
Into old aisles where the past is all to him,
    Close as his shade can do,
Always lacking the power to call to him,
    Near as I reach thereto!

What a good haunter I am, O tell him!
  Quickly make him know
If he but sigh since my loss befell him
  Straight to his side I go.
Tell him a faithful one is doing
  All that love can do
Still that his path may be worth pursuing,
  And to bring peace thereto.

The Voice

WOMAN much missed, how you call to me, call to me,
Saying that now you are not as you were
When you had changed from the one who was all to me,
But as at first, when our day was fair.

Can it be you that I hear? Let me view you, then,
Standing as when I drew near to the town
Where you would wait for me: yes, as I knew you then,
Even to the original air-blue gown!

Or is it only the breeze, in its listlessness
Travelling across the wet mead to me here,
You being ever dissolved to wan wistlessness,
Heard no more again far or near?

  Thus I; faltering forward,
  Leaves around me falling,
Wind oozing thin through the thorn from norward,
  And the woman calling.

December 1912

A Dream or No

WHY go to Saint-Juliot? What's Juliot to me?
      Some strange necromancy
      But charmed me to fancy
That much of my life claims the spot as its key.

Yes. I have had dreams of that place in the West,
      And a maiden abiding
      Thereat as in hiding;
Fair-eyed and white-shouldered, broad-browed and
    brown-tressed.

And of how, coastward bound on a night long ago,
      There lonely I found her,
      The sea-birds around her,
And other than nigh things uncaring to know.

So sweet her life there (in my thought has it seemed)
      That quickly she drew me
      To take her unto me,
And lodge her long years with me. Such have I dreamed.

But nought of that maid from Saint-Juliot I see;
      Can she ever have been here,
      And shed her life's sheen here,
The woman I thought a long housemate with me?

Does there even a place like Saint-Juliot exist?
      Or a Vallency Valley
      With stream and leafed alley,
Or Beeny, or Bos with its flounce flinging mist?

February 1913

After a Journey

HERETO I come to view a voiceless ghost;
　　Whither, O whither will its whim now draw me?
Up the cliff, down, till I'm lonely, lost,
　　And the unseen waters' ejaculations awe me.
Where you will next be there's no knowing,
　　Facing round about me everywhere,
　　　　With your nut-coloured hair,
And gray eyes, and rose-flush coming and going.

Yes: I have re-entered your olden haunts at last;
　　Through the years, through the dead scenes I have tracked
　　　　you;
What have you now found to say of our past –
　　Scanned across the dark space wherein I have lacked you?
Summer gave us sweets, but autumn wrought division?
　　Things were not lastly as firstly well
　　　　With us twain, you tell?
But all's closed now, despite Time's derision.

I see what you are doing: you are leading me on
　　To the spots we knew when we haunted here together,
The waterfall, above which the mist-bow shone
　　At the then fair hour in the then fair weather,
And the cave just under, with a voice still so hollow
　　That it seems to call out to me from forty years ago,
　　　　When you were all aglow,
And not the thin ghost that I now frailly follow!

Ignorant of what there is flitting here to see,
　　The waked birds preen and the seals flop lazily;
Soon you will have, Dear, to vanish from me,
　　For the stars close their shutters and the dawn whitens
　　　　hazily.
Trust me, I mind not, though Life lours,
　　The bringing me here; nay, bring me here again!
　　　　I am just the same as when
Our days were a joy, and our paths through flowers.

Pentargan Bay

Beeny Cliff

March 1870–March 1913

I

O THE opal and the sapphire of that wandering western sea,
And the woman riding high above with bright hair flapping
    free –
The woman whom I loved so, and who loyally loved me.

II

The pale mews plained below us, and the waves seemed far
    away
In a nether sky, engrossed in saying their ceaseless babbling
    say,
As we laughed light-heartedly aloft on that clear-sunned
    March day.

III

A little cloud then cloaked us, and there flew an irised rain,
And the Atlantic dyed its levels with a dull misfeatured stain,
And then the sun burst out again, and purples prinked the
    main.

IV

– Still in all its chasmal beauty bulks old Beeny to the sky,
And shall she and I not go there once again now March is
    nigh,
And the sweet things said in that March say anew there by
    and by?

V

What if still in chasmal beauty looms that wild weird western
    shore,
The woman now is – elsewhere – whom the ambling pony
    bore,
And nor knows nor cares for Beeny, and will laugh there
    nevermore.

At Castle Boterel

As I drive to the junction of lane and highway,
    And the drizzle bedrenches the waggonette,
I look behind at the fading byway,
    And see on its slope, now glistening wet,
        Distinctly yet

Myself and a girlish form benighted
    In dry March weather. We climb the road
Beside a chaise. We had just alighted
    To ease the sturdy pony's load
        When he sighed and slowed.

What we did as we climbed, and what we talked of
    Matters not much, nor to what it led, –
Something that life will not be balked of
    Without rude reason till hope is dead,
        And feeling fled.

It filled but a minute. But was there ever
    A time of such quality, since or before,
In that hill's story? To one mind never,
    Though it has been climbed, foot-swift, foot-sore,
        By thousands more.

Primaeval rocks form the road's steep border,
    And much have they faced there, first and last,
Of the transitory in Earth's long order;
    But what they record in colour and cast
        Is – that we two passed.

And to me, though Time's unflinching rigour,
    In mindless rote, has ruled from sight
The substance now, one phantom figure
    Remains on the slope, as when that night
        Saw us alight.

I look and see it there, shrinking, shrinking,
    I look back at it amid the rain
For the very last time; for my sand is sinking,
    And I shall traverse old love's domain
        Never again.

March 1913

Places

NOBODY says: Ah, that is the place
Where chanced, in the hollow of years ago,
What none of the Three Towns cared to know –
The birth of a little girl of grace –
The sweetest the house saw, first or last;
      Yet it was so
      On that day long past.

Nobody thinks: There, there she lay
In a room by the Hoe, like the bud of a flower,
And listened, just after the bedtime hour,
To the stammering chimes that used to play
The quaint Old Hundred-and-Thirteenth tune
      In Saint Andrew's tower
      Night, morn, and noon.

Nobody calls to mind that here
Upon Boterel Hill, where the waggoners skid,
With cheeks whose airy flush outbid
Fresh fruit in bloom, and free of fear,
She cantered down, as if she must fall
      (Though she never did),
      To the charm of all.

Nay: one there is to whom these things,
That nobody else's mind calls back,
Have a savour that scenes in being lack,
And a presence more than the actual brings;
To whom to-day is beneaped and stale,
      And its urgent clack
      But a vapid tale.

Plymouth, March 1913

The Phantom Horsewoman

I

QUEER are the ways of a man I know:
        He comes and stands
        In a careworn craze,
        And looks at the sands
        And the seaward haze
        With moveless hands
        And face and gaze,
        Then turns to go . . .
And what does he see when he gazes so?

II

They say he sees as an instant thing
        More clear than to-day,
        A sweet soft scene
        That was once in play
        By that briny green;
        Yes, notes alway
        Warm, real, and keen,
        What his back years bring –
A phantom of his own figuring.

III

Of this vision of his they might say more:
        Not only there
        Does he see this sight,
        But everywhere
        In his brain – day, night,
        As if on the air
        It were drawn rose bright –
        Yea, far from that shore
Does he carry this vision of heretofore:

IV

A ghost-girl-rider. And though, toil-tried,
    He withers daily,
    Time touches her not,
    But she still rides gaily
    In his rapt thought
    On that shagged and shaly
    Atlantic spot,
    And as when first eyed
Draws rein and sings to the swing of the tide.

1913

Where the Picnic Was

WHERE we made the fire
In the summer time
Of branch and briar
On the hill to the sea,
I slowly climb
Through winter mire,
And scan and trace
The forsaken place
Quite readily.

Now a cold wind blows,
And the grass is gray,
But the spot still shows
As a burnt circle – aye,
And stick-ends, charred,
Still strew the sward
Whereon I stand,
Last relic of the band
Who came that day!

Yes, I am here
Just as last year,
And the sea breathes brine
From its strange straight line

Up hither, the same
As when we four came.
– But two have wandered far
From this grassy rise
Into urban roar
Where no picnics are,
And one – has shut her eyes
For evermore.

He Prefers Her Earthly

THIS after-sunset is a sight for seeing,
Cliff-heads of craggy cloud surrounding it.
  – And dwell you in that glory-show?
You may; for there are strange strange things in being,
    Stranger than I know.

Yet if that chasm of splendour claim your presence
Which glows between the ash cloud and the dun,
  How changed must be your mortal mould!
Changed to a firmament-riding earthless essence
    From what you were of old:

All too unlike the fond and fragile creature
Then known to me. . . . Well, shall I say it plain?
  I would not have you thus and there,
But still would grieve on, missing you, still feature
    You as the one you were.

Without, Not Within Her

IT was what you bore with you, Woman,
    Not inly were,
That throned you from all else human,
    However fair!

It was that strange freshness you carried
        Into a soul
Whereon no thought of yours tarried
        Two moments at all.

And out from his spirit flew death,
        And bale, and ban,
Like the corn-chaff under the breath
        Of the winnowing-fan.

A Night in November

I MARKED when the weather changed,
And the panes began to quake,
And the winds rose up and ranged,
That night, lying half-awake.

Dead leaves blew into my room,
And alighted upon my bed,
And a tree declared to the gloom
Its sorrow that they were shed.

One leaf of them touched my hand,
And I thought that it was you
There stood as you used to stand,
And saying at last you knew!

    (?) 1913

'My Spirit Will Not Haunt the Mound'

MY spirit will not haunt the mound
        Above my breast,
But travel, memory-possessed,
To where my tremulous being found
        Life largest, best.

My phantom-footed shape will go
    When nightfall grays
Hither and thither along the ways
I and another used to know
    In backward days.

And there you'll find me, if a jot
    You still should care
For me, and for my curious air;
If otherwise, then I shall not,
    For you, be there.

An Upbraiding

Now I am dead you sing to me
    The songs we used to know,
But while I lived you had no wish
    Or care for doing so.

Now I am dead you come to me
    In the moonlight, comfortless;
Ah, what would I have given alive
    To win such tenderness!

When you are dead, and stand to me
    Not differenced, as now,
But like again, will you be cold
    As when we lived, or how?

'The Curtains Now Are Drawn'

(*Song*)

I

THE curtains now are drawn,
And the spindrift strikes the glass,
Blown up the jaggèd pass
By the surly salt sou'-west,
And the sneering glare is gone
Behind the yonder crest,
    While she sings to me:
'O the dream that thou art my Love, be it thine,
And the dream that I am thy Love, be it mine,
And death may come, but loving is divine.'

II

I stand here in the rain,
With its smite upon her stone,
And the grasses that have grown
Over women, children, men,
And their texts that 'Life is vain;'
But I hear the notes as when
    Once she sang to me:
'O the dream that thou art my Love, be it thine,
And the dream that I am thy Love, be it mine,
And death may come, but loving is divine.'

1913

The Dream Is – Which?

I AM laughing by the brook with her,
    Splashed in its tumbling stir;
And then it is a blankness looms
    As if I walked not there,
Nor she, but found me in haggard rooms,
    And treading a lonely stair.

With radiant cheeks and rapid eyes
  We sit where none espies;
Till a harsh change comes edging in
  As no such scene were there,
But winter, and I were bent and thin,
  And cinder-gray my hair.

We dance in heys around the hall,
  Weightless as thistleball;
And then a curtain drops between,
  As if I danced not there,
But wandered through a mounded green
  To find her, I knew where.

March 1913

The Figure in the Scene

IT pleased her to step in front and sit
  Where the cragged slope was green,
While I stood back that I might pencil it
  With her amid the scene;
    Till it gloomed and rained;
But I kept on, despite the drifting wet
  That fell and stained
My draught, leaving for curious quizzings yet
  The blots engrained.

And thus I drew her there alone,
  Seated amid the gauze
Of moisture, hooded, only her outline shown,
  With rainfall marked across.
    – Soon passed our stay;
Yet her rainy form is the Genius still of the spot,
  Immutable, yea,
Though the place now knows her no more, and has known
      her not
  Ever since that day.

From an old note

The Marble Tablet

THERE it stands, though alas, what a little of her
　　Shows in its cold white look!
Not her glance, glide, or smile; not a tittle of her
　　Voice like the purl of a brook;
　　　Not her thoughts, that you read like a book.

It may stand for her once in November
　　When first she breathed, witless of all;
Or in heavy years she would remember
　　When circumstance held her in thrall;
　　　Or at last, when she answered her call!

Nothing more. The still marble, date-graven,
　　Gives all that it can, tersely lined;
That one has at length found the haven
　　Which every one other will find;
　　　With silence on what shone behind.

St Juliot: 8 September 1916

The Shadow on the Stone

I WENT by the Druid stone
That broods in the garden white and lone,
And I stopped and looked at the shifting shadows
　That at some moments fall thereon
　From the tree hard by with a rhythmic swing,
　And they shaped in my imagining
To the shade that a well-known head and shoulders
　Threw there when she was gardening.

I thought her behind my back,
Yea, her I long had learned to lack,
And I said: 'I am sure you are standing behind me,
Though how do you get into this old track?'
And there was no sound but the fall of a leaf
As a sad response; and to keep down grief
I would not turn my head to discover
That there was nothing in my belief.

Yet I wanted to look and see
That nobody stood at the back of me;
But I thought once more: 'Nay, I'll not unvision
A shape which, somehow, there may be.'
So I went on softly from the glade,
And left her behind me throwing her shade,
As she were indeed an apparition –
My head unturned lest my dream should fade.

Begun 1913: finished 1916

Ten Years Since

'TIS ten years since
I saw her on the stairs,
Heard her in house-affairs,
And listened to her cares;
And the trees are ten feet taller,
And the sunny spaces smaller
Whose bloomage would enthrall her;
And the piano wires are rustier,
The smell of bindings mustier,
And lofts and lumber dustier
Than when, with casual look
And ear, light note I took
Of what shut like a book
Those ten years since!

Nov. 1922

During Wind and Rain

THEY sing their dearest songs –
He, she, all of them – yea,
Treble and tenor and bass,
 And one to play;
With the candles mooning each face. . . .
 Ah, no; the years O!
How the sick leaves reel down in throngs!

They clear the creeping moss –
Elder and juniors – aye,
Making the pathways neat
 And the garden gay;
And they build a shady seat. . . .
 Ah, no; the years, the years;
See, the white storm-birds wing across!

They are blithely breakfasting all –
Men and maidens – yea,
Under the summer tree,
 With a glimpse of the bay,
While pet fowl come to the knee. . . .
 Ah, no; the years O!
And the rotten rose is ript from the wall.

They change to a high new house,
He, she, all of them – aye,
Clocks and carpets and chairs
 On the lawn all day,
And brightest things that are theirs. . . .
 Ah, no; the years, the years;
Down their carved names the rain-drop ploughs.

Notes

CHILDHOOD AMONG THE FERNS (p. **1**). During the years 1925–8 H. was consulting diaries and notebooks for *The Early Life* and *The Later Years*. Autobiographical equivalent in the *Life*, 15–16. Cf. also *Jude* (Pt. I, ch. ii). The birthplace at Higher Bockhampton is still surrounded by a profusion of ferns.

AFTERNOON SERVICE AT MELLSTOCK (p. **1**). 'Mellstock' = Stinsford. The image of swaying trees entered in a notebook 1871. Cf. similar scene in *Desperate Remedies*, ch. xii, 8.

TO AN UNBORN PAUPER CHILD (p. **2**). A note on the MS reads ' "She must go to the Union-house to have her baby." Casterbridge [Dorchester] Petty Sessions'. For the same view of life's prospects for paupers cf. *Tess*, ch. iii; *Jude*, Pt. VI, ch. ii. 'teens' = sorrows.

THE SUBALTERNS (p. **3**). For the idea of hostile forces being themselves helplessly regimented, cf. the words of the Shade of the Earth at the opening of *The Dynasts*. 'shorn one' – cf. proverb 'God tempers the wind to the shorn lamb'.

DISCOURAGEMENT (p. **4**). Dated 1865–7 in MS. The phrase 'naturing Nature' translates *natura naturans* which H. contemplated as subtitle at proof stage: the medieval concept of Nature herself developing God's purpose. Here, however, she is seen in secular, Darwinian terms. Any evolutionary tendency towards the perfection of man is warped by his subjection, in mating, to small accidents of physical attraction and social status.

REVULSION (p. **5**). 'junctive law' = marriage.

SHE, TO HIM I, III (pp. **5, 6**). H. said that the four sonnets published were 'part of a much larger number which perished'.

HER DILEMMA (p. **6**). H.'s cross-section drawing matches the 'insight' of the poem, revealing coffins and skeletons under the lovers' feet. Consideration of his impending death unfairly 'conditions' her to lie.

IN TENEBRIS I, II, III (pp. **7, 8, 9**). Title = 'In Darkness'. The three Latin epigraphs are from St Jerome's translation of the Psalms in the

Vulgate Bible. The equivalent Authorised Version translations are: 'My heart is smitten, and withered like grass' (Psalm 102); 'I looked on my right hand, and beheld, but there was no man that would know me . . . no man cared for my soul' (Psalm 142); 'Woe is me that I sojourn in Mesech, that I dwell in the tents of Kedar. My soul hath long dwelt with him that hateth peace' (Psalm 120). IN TENEBRIS II: 'one born out of due time' = St Paul's self-description in I Corinthians 15:8.   IN TENEBRIS III: the image in the last-but-two line is from Revelation 10:9–10 (an angel offering John a book): 'And he said unto me, Take it and eat it up; and it shall make thy belly bitter, but it shall be in thy mouth sweet as honey'.

THE DEAD MAN WALKING (p. 11). Dated 1896 in MS.   Stanza 7: the death of 'my friend' was probably that of Horace Moule (suicide 1873) and the 'kinsfolk' lost included H.'s father (d. 1892).   Stanza 8: probably a reference to Emma's growing bitterness.

THE SOMETHING THAT SAVED HIM (p. 12). 'Cit' = citizen.

YELL'HAM-WOOD'S STORY (p. 13). Yellowham Wood (the location of many scenes in the novels) is between Puddletown and Dorchester. The other two woods (both of fir trees) are also near H.'s birthplace.

HAP (p. 14). H. objected to early misreadings of the poem. Its emphasis is on the indifference, not the evil, of chance. 'unblooms' = does not bloom at all. 'for gladness' = instead of gladness.

THE CONVERGENCE OF THE TWAIN (p. 14). First published in the programme of a matinée in aid of the *Titanic* Disaster Fund at Covent Garden. The *Titanic*, claimed to be 'unsinkable', had sunk after striking an iceberg on its maiden voyage on 15 April 1912, with a loss of 1,513 lives. Newspaper reports had described the ship as the most luxuriously appointed vessel ever launched.   'thrid' = wind through.

GOD-FORGOTTEN (p. 16). The poem refers to earth's Fall in Eden – from 'doing as it durst' – divorcing it however from all other Christian belief about the event.

A PLAINT TO MAN (p. 17). Titled 'The Plaint of a Puppet' in MS, the puppet being God, existing only in the sense of being invented by man, and subject therefore to man's particular needs. Stanza 4: 'phasm' = a ghostly appearance, activated as if on a screen by the 'showman' (priest). 'the deicide eyes of seers' = rationalist philosophies that now kill even the need for a god.

A CATHEDRAL FAÇADE AT MIDNIGHT (p. **19**). Dated 1897 in MS, it matches a journal entry describing a visit to Salisbury Cathedral in August of that year. The moonlight comes to represent the light of Reason as it falls on the symbols of Christianity.

DRUMMER HODGE (p. **20**). The poem refers to the Boer War (1899–1902). On the identification of the dead drummer with the physical world cf. Wordsworth's 'A slumber did my spirit seal' and Housman's 'The night is freezing fast'. 'kopje' (small hill), 'veldt' (wild grass-land), 'karoo' (high waterless plateau) are Dutch-South African names.

THE SOULS OF THE SLAIN (p. **21**). The souls are of soldiers killed in the Boer War. Portland Bill (known locally as the 'Isle') is the southern-most part of England 'roughly, on a line drawn from South Africa to the middle of the United Kingdom' (H.'s note on first printing). 'bent-bearded' = covered with wind-bent grass. 'mighty-vanned' = with large wings. 'turreted lantern' = the lighthouse on Portland Bill. 'Like the Pentecost Wind' – a reference to Acts 2:1–2: 'And when the day of Pentecost was fully come . . . suddenly there came a sound from heaven as of a rushing mighty wind'.

THE MAN HE KILLED (p. **24**). The speaker is a soldier returned from the Boer War. 'nipperkin' = small drinking measure.

CHANNEL FIRING (p. **25**). The poem (written April 1914) was prophetic without actually forecasting the outbreak of war three months later. 'glebe' = land tied to a church living. A 'Parson Thirdly' also appears in *Far from the Madding Crowd*. 'Stourton Tower' commemorates King Alfred's victory over the Danes in a battle of 879; along with Camelot (King Arthur's Court) and Stonehenge it suggests, historically and mythically, earlier 'civilizations' of blood and war.

IN TIME OF 'THE BREAKING OF NATIONS' (p. **26**). Though written during the 1914–18 war, the idea had occurred to H. in 1870, during the Franco-Prussian War. The quoted phrase in the title refers to

Jeremiah 51:20 (God's judgment against Babylon) 'for with thee will I break in pieces the nations'. The passage however also speaks of the breaking of 'the young man and the maid' and 'the husbandman and his yoke of oxen' (verses 22–3). 'couch-grass' = grass-weed.

'I MET A MAN' (p. **27**). 'Like Moses after Sinai' – a reference to Exodus 34:29: Moses having brought down the tables of the Commandments, 'the skin of his face' shining. 'Cockers' = arrangers of cock-fights. 'death-mains' = (from cockfighting) a fight to the death. The reference to Saul evokes I Samuel 15:11, Jehovah lamenting 'that I have set up Saul to be king: for he is turned back from following me'.

A NEW YEAR'S EVE IN WAR TIME (p. **28**). 'Hand-hid' – because the hour-hand is covered by the minute-hand at midnight. H. claimed that the incident of hearing a horse galloping past at midnight of the New Year was true. 'Death astride' – a reference to the 'pale horse' of Revelation 6:8 (for last stanza see also Revelation 6:2–5 and Revelation 8).

ACCORDING TO THE MIGHTY WORKING (p. **31**). Title – from the Burial Service (words from Ephesians 1:19: 'And what is the exceeding greatness of his power to us-ward who believe, according to the working of his mighty power'). A reference in the *Life*, 388, links the poem to the movement to re-establish Palestine as a home for the Jews, which H. supported. Even after the cessation of war, 'this hid riot, Change' continues – a reference to the Heraclitean idea of eternal flux. 'moiling' = drudging toil.

THE RESPECTABLE BURGHER (p. **32**). Subtitle – the 'Higher Criticism' sought to submit the Bible to rational interpretation based on the disciplines of history, linguistics and science. Its excesses are satirized as much as the speaker's middle-class dependence on a literal reading of the Bible in the first place. For H. the moral truths of the Bible are not so easily removed or ignored. He sustains the satiric note on one rhyme throughout. 'Piombo' = Sebastiano Luciani, a Renaissance Italian artist, whose painting 'The Raising of Lazarus' is in the National Gallery.

YULETIDE IN A YOUNGER WORLD (p. **33**). 'still small voices' – a reference to H.'s favourite passage in the Bible (I Kings 19:11–12) ending 'and after the fire a still small voice' (Elijah hearing God's voice in the wilderness).

A SIGN-SEEKER (p. 33). The first five stanzas list empirically observable facts which, however, do not include signs that a cosmic eye is kept on the world's evils or that individuals survive death.

THE IMPERCIPIENT (p. 35). Titled in the MS 'The Agnostic (Evensong: —— Cathedral)'. The accompanying drawing in *Wessex Poems* is of the nave of Salisbury Cathedral.

THE OXEN (p. 36). The legend of animals kneeling on Christmas Eve is comically referred to in Dairyman Crick's story about William Dewy in *Tess*, ch. xvii.   'barton' = farmyard.

'I LOOK INTO MY GLASS' (p. 37). Cf. Pierston's thoughts on the same theme in *The Well-Beloved*, Pt. II, ch. xii and Pt. III, chs. iv and vii.

DRINKING SONG (p. 39). Subtitle suggested in MS – 'on Great Thoughts belittled'.   'Thales' (fl. *c.* 580 BC): Greek mathematician and philosopher, by reputation important for developing scientific inquiry away from myth; his view of the universe however remained earth-centred. 'Copernicus' (1473–1543): Polish astronomer who discovered that the Earth and other planets moved round the Sun. 'Hume' (1711–76): Scottish empiricist philosopher whose emphasis on natural laws queries the likelihood of miracles. 'Darwin' (1809–82): English biologist whose theories of plant and animal evolution had a profound effect on H.   'Doctor Cheyne' (1841–1915): English biblical scholar who denied the Virgin Birth of Christ.   'Einstein' (1875–1955): German-Swiss physicist whose theory of Relativity transformed Newtonian understanding of physical laws.

'WE ARE GETTING TO THE END' (p. 42). 'not warely' = not from their own conscious choosing.

THE ABSOLUTE EXPLAINS (p. 43). The explanation seeks to get rid of the linear notion of Time: people and experiences do not pass away but exist in an eternal present. Stanza XIV refers to Einstein's Relativity theory. The individual woman whom the poet has asked about is probably his first wife (d. 1912).

'LET ME ENJOY' (p. 46). The poem is a prelude to 'A Set of Country

Songs', seventeen in number, depicting rural Dorset scenes and characters.

HE RESOLVES TO SAY NO MORE (p. 47). 'Pale Horse' – see Revelation 6:8, 'And I looked, and behold a pale horse: and his name that sat on him was Death, and Hell followed with him'.   'Magians' = wise men.

NATURE'S QUESTIONING (p. 50). H. claimed that early dawn was for him a period of moral depression.   First two stanzas – cf. Journal entry (Feb. 1897): 'In spite of myself I cannot help noticing countenances and tempers in objects of scenery, eg., trees, hills, houses'.

DOMICILIUM (p. 51). Written 1857–60. First published as pamphlet (1916); not collected, but reprinted in The Early Life (1928). Cf. opening chapter of The Return of the Native. The house is H.'s birthplace at Higher Bockhampton.

A BIRD-SCENE AT A RURAL DWELLING (p. 52). H.'s birthplace at Higher Bockhampton.

AT MIDDLE-FIELD GATE IN FEBRUARY (p. 52). The 'Middle' fields lay between the North and South fields along the lane near H.'s birthplace.

AT DAY-CLOSE IN NOVEMBER (p. 54). The scene is Max Gate.

FOUR IN THE MORNING (p. 55). The young H. used to rise early to study Latin and Greek before leaving for work in an architect's office in Dorchester.

THE SHEEP-BOY (p. 55). The note 'On Rainbarrows' refers to the three tumuli on Puddletown ('Egdon') Heath near H.'s birthplace.   'Draäts' = Dorset dialect for wet winds.   'Pokeswell Hills' = Poxwell Hills, five miles to the south.   'moving pillar of cloud' – that which guided the Israelites in Exodus 13:21.   'Kite-Hill' – south of Puddletown.   'viewless' = invisible.

A WET AUGUST (p. 57). 'that August' – of H.'s second visit to Emma in Cornwall in 1870.

WE FIELD-WOMEN (p. 60). Closely associated with Tess's experiences at Flintcomb-Ash Farm in Tess of the D'Urbervilles (chs. xlii and xliii). Tess, however, did not return with the other women to Talbothays Dairy (stanza 3).

THE YEAR'S AWAKENING (p. 63). 'Fishes ... Ram' = the zodiacal periods.

AT A LUNAR ECLIPSE (p. 64). MS dated '186–'. Clym Yeobright contemplates human ambition while watching the moon's eclipse in *The Return of the Native* (Book Third, ch. iv).

ONCE AT SWANAGE (p. 64). H. and his first wife lived at Swanage August 1875–March 1876.

SHUT OUT THAT MOON (p. 65). J. O. Bailey notes a Dorset superstition about the evil portent of seeing the moon through glass. 'Lady's Chair' = Cassiopeia's Chair, a constellation in the northern hemisphere.

THE DARKLING THRUSH (p. 66). Title – relevant uses of the word 'darkling' occur in Milton's *Paradise Lost* (III, 39), Keats's 'Ode to a Nightingale' and Arnold's 'Dover Beach'. Original title – 'By the Century's Deathbed'. 'bine-stems' = flexible shoots of climbing plants.

BIRDS AT WINTER NIGHTFALL (p. 67). The 'triolet' form requires the first line to appear three times, but with different syntactic meanings.

AFTERWARDS (p. 67). 'postern' = back or side door. 'dewfall-hawk' = the nightjar. 'quittance' = technically, release from obligation.

A SHEEP FAIR (p. 73). 'Pummery' = Poundbury, a hill with ancient earthworks, overlooking the Frome river north-west of Dorchester.

LAST LOOK ROUND ST MARTIN'S FAIR (p. 74). Martinstown (originally St Martin), a village south-west of Dorchester. 'heathcroppers' = wild ponies. 'Great Forest' = New Forest.

COMING UP OXFORD STREET: EVENING (p. 75). The second stanza was originally in the first person. The date was some three months before H. finally abandoned his architectural career in London.

THE NEWCOMER'S WIFE (p. 77). The image of the dead man 'with crabs upon his face' also occurs when Pierston contemplates suicide in the novel *The Well-Beloved* (Part First, ch. vii).

CYNIC'S EPITAPH (p. 77). Originally a companion-piece to 'Epitaph on a Pessimist'.

THE BIRD-CATCHER'S BOY (p. 78). 'in Babylon/Captive' – cf. Psalms

137:1–3): 'By the rivers of Babylon, there we sat down, yea, we wept, when we remembered Zion . . . For there they that carried us away captive required of us a song'. 'hoy' = small, unrigged vessel.

MIDNIGHT ON THE GREAT WESTERN (p. 80). The description has a close equivalent in that of Little Father Time travelling to Aldbrickham on the same railway line (*Jude the Obscure*, Pt. V, ch. iii).

AT THE RAILWAY STATION, UPWAY (p. 81). Upwey [sic] is a village south of Dorchester. The railway continued to the Isle of Portland, where there was a prison.

THE WHITEWASHED WALL (p. 82). Cf. Swithin's grandmother's refusal to erase the charcoal scratches he had made on the wall of his room in *Two on a Tower* (ch. xxxviii).

ONE WE KNEW (p. 82). The subject is Mary Head Hardy, the poet's paternal grandmother. Cf. Swithin's grandmother in *Two on a Tower* (ch. ii).

A CHURCH ROMANCE (p. 84). The man and woman were H.'s parents.

AFTER THE LAST BREATH (p. 84). The dead woman is H.'s mother.

LOGS ON THE HEARTH (p. 85). On memories of Mary, the elder of H.'s two sisters, and his favourite.

MOLLY GONE (p. 86). Molly = H.'s sister Mary. 'the town by the sea' = Weymouth. The other places are north and west from Dorchester.

STANDING BY THE MANTELPIECE (p. 87). 'H.M.M.' = Horace Moseley Moule, H.'s early friend and mentor, who committed suicide at Cambridge, 1873. Folk superstition claimed that shroud-shaped candle-wax presaged death; moulding it with the fingers is a sign of accepting the omen. Horace Moule is the speaker. He is addressing a woman, possibly the 'un-named lady of title' to whom (according to Sir Sydney Cockerell, quoting Hardy) Moule had become engaged. On one occasion Moule had apparently disgraced her with his drunkenness. The fourth stanza, however, hints at something deeper.

BARTHÉLÉMON AT VAUXHALL (p. 88). 'Awake my soul' was one of H.'s favourite hymns. The words by Bishop Thomas Ken (1637–1711) were written *c*. 1674 and the music by Barthélémon (1741–1808) *c*. 1780. Vauxhall Gardens (closed 1859) had been a place for popular entertainment since the mid-seventeenth century.

THE LAST SIGNAL (p. **88**). William Barnes had been a close friend. He had run a school next door to the Dorchester architect's office where H. was apprenticed 1856–62 and his church and rectory were very close to Max Gate, H.'s home from 1885. The influence on Barnes's poetry of Welsh poetic devices like internal rhymes and alliterative patterns is reflected in H.'s own poem.

THE SCHRECKHORN (p. **89**). Leslie Stephen (1832–1904), Virginia Woolf's father, had been a close friend and influence since 1872 when, as editor, he had offered H. serial publication in the *Cornhill* magazine. Stephen had been the first man to climb the Schreckhorn peak in the Swiss Alps, which the Hardys visited in 1897.

THE CURATE'S KINDNESS (p. **94**). There was a 'Union' workhouse at Dorchester. 'Pummery (Poundbury) or Ten-Hatches Weir' – both on the river Frome near Dorchester.

TO C.F.H. (p. **99**). For H.'s godchild, Caroline Fox Hanbury, of Kingston Maurward House, Stinsford.

AN ANCIENT TO ANCIENTS (p. **99**). Stanza 4 – *The Bohemian Girl* was an opera (1843) by Balfe. Stanza 6 – 'she who voiced those rhymes' recalls a day in 1870 when H. and his first wife had read Tennyson in the garden of St Juliot rectory. Stanza 7 – 'Aïdes' (Hades) = Greek king of the underworld.

BEREFT (p. **101**). 'Durnover Lea' = Fordington Moor, east of Dorchester.

THE BURGHERS (p. **105**). 'Grey's to Dammer's Crest' = hills east and west of Dorchester (the town itself, and a particular house, are also carefully visualized). 'Furnace' – see Daniel 7:3–25. 'haw' = a field. Cf. Phillotson's magnanimity in releasing Sue from marriage in *Jude the Obscure* (Pt. IV, ch. iv).

THE DANCE AT THE PHOENIX (p. **107**). The setting is Dorchester ('Casterbridge'), again very carefully visualized. 'apple-blooth' = apple blossom. 'Parrett', 'Yeo' and 'Tone' are rivers. 'Sirius' = the brightest star (Dog Star). 'Charles's Wain' = a constellation. 'durn' = door-post.

A TRAMPWOMAN'S TRAGEDY (p. **116**). 'Sedge-Moor' = where King James II defeated the Duke of Monmouth, 1665. 'tor' = rocky hill-top. 'Ivel-chester' = Ilchester, ten miles south of Glastonbury ('Glaston').

THE BALLAD OF LOVE'S SKELETON (p. **120**). The man is a baron of King George III's court. The King made regular summer visits to Weymouth 1789–1805.

WESSEX HEIGHTS (p. **124**). The four 'heights' are like four corners to the main part of 'Wessex' lying north of Dorchester, and each is an ancient hill-fort. H.'s second wife said that the poem involves four 'actual women'. Speculations have been as follows: H.'s first wife, Emma (stanza 2); H.'s mother (stanza 5); Tryphena Sparks, d. 1890 (stanza 6); and, less speculatively, Mrs Florence Henniker, who returned friendship for H.'s love (stanza 6). The poem (1896) was affected by the public reaction to *Jude the Obscure*.

ROME: THE VATICAN: SALA DELLE MUSE (p. **128**). The Hardys had visited Italy, spring 1887. The theme of the unity of the various arts was possibly influenced by criticism of H.'s switch from fiction to poetry. 'Be not perturbed' – a favourite aphorism from Marcus Aurelius. 'becall' = insult verbally.

LAUSANNE: IN GIBBON'S OLD GARDEN (p. **131**). The Milton reference is to *The Doctrine and Discipline of Divorce*. H. had the reception of his novels, especially *Jude the Obscure*, in mind.

ZERMATT: TO THE MATTERHORN (p. **131**). The tragic 1865 ascent of the mountain had been led by E. M. Whymper, whom H. met in 1894. 'Joshua' – see Joshua 10:13. 'Caesar' – see *Julius Caesar* II, ii, 19–21. 'that Noon' – at Christ's crucifixion (Mark 15:33).

AFTER THE FAIR (p. **137**). 'stammering chimes' – before the Great War, the bells of St Peter's Church, Dorchester also played secular tunes. 'drongs' = narrow country lanes.

BEYOND THE LAST LAMP (p. **144**). Tess and Angel Clare make a similar impression on a passer-by in *Tess of the D'Urbervilles*, ch. xxxv.

FRIENDS BEYOND (p. **145**). 'Tranter' = carrier. 'stillicide' = dripping of water. 'Ye mid' = you may. 'hold . . . in fee' = inherit. 'grin-terns' = granary bins. 'Trine' = Trinity.

TRANSFORMATIONS (p. 147). 'the fair girl long ago' = Louisa Harding, one of H.'s boyhood loves, daughter of a Stinsford farmer.

THE CHOIRMASTER'S BURIAL (p. 148). The choirmaster was H.'s grandfather. 'tenor man' = H.'s father, tenor violinist in the Stinsford Church choir.

VOICES FROM THINGS GROWING IN A CHURCHYARD (p. 149). Only 'Lady Gertrude' is not identifiable via Stinsford Church graves or records. Voss appears in *Under the Greenwood Tree* (Part the First, ch. iv). 'withwind' = clematis called 'virgin's bower'.

A SPELLBOUND PALACE (p. 151). 'King' = Henry VIII. 'his Minister' = Cardinal Wolsey, who had built Hampton Court. He gave it to Henry in 1526.

NEAR LANIVET, 1872 (p. 155). The woman was Emma, H.'s first wife. The poet stressed that the incident did actually happen. Lanivet is near Bodmin, Cornwall, where in 1872 they visited Emma's father, hostile to their engagement.

'IN THE SEVENTIES' (p. 156). Epigraph – from the Vulgate Bible, Job 12:4 (Authorised Version: 'I am as one mocked of his neighbour'). The theme is probably the inner hopes (literary success and his love for Emma) that 'immuned' him against outward disappointments in the early 1870s.

EXEUNT OMNES (p. 157). The date noted was H.'s seventy-third birthday.

HEIRESS AND ARCHITECT (p. 160). 'ogive-work' = pointed arches. 'engrailed' = given a decorative border.

SELF-UNCONSCIOUS (p. 163). H.'s note 'Near Bossiney' refers to a village near Boscastle, thus connecting the poem to one of his early visits to Emma in Cornwall in 1870. Already present but unrealized were the ingredients (possibly of personality) that made the relationship grow bitter in the 1890s.

OVERLOOKING THE RIVER STOUR (p. 169). The MS dates the poem's event as '(1877)'. From summer 1876 to March 1878 the Hardys lived at Sturminster Newton, Dorset. H. called that period an 'idyll ... Our happiest time' – but during it, he now feels, he neglected Emma's individual emotional needs.

THE MUSICAL BOX (p. 170). See previous note on 'Overlooking the River Stour'.

ON STURMINSTER FOOT-BRIDGE (p. 171). See note on 'Overlooking the River Stour' above. 'eyot-withies' – eyot = small island in a river, withies = willows.

A TWO-YEARS' IDYLL (p. 172). See note on 'Overlooking the River Stour' above.

THE INTERLOPER (p. 173). There was a background of mental instability in Emma Hardy's family. Here the spectre of insanity is seen as hanging over Emma herself in scenes suggesting Cornwall (stanza 1) and Sturminster Newton (stanza 2).

AT A BRIDAL (p. 175). Nature's indifference and 'class' motives in marriage frustrate the improvement of the human race through the pairing of ideal partners. 'unknows' = does not know at all.

TO LOUISA IN THE LANE (p. 175). To one of H.'s early loves, Louisa Harding, daughter of a Stinsford farmer who considered H. socially unsuitable.

NEUTRAL TONES (p. 176). For similar bleak landscapes indelibly impressed on the mind in an emotional crisis cf. the experience of Gabriel Oak in *Far from the Madding Crowd* (ch. v) and that of Knight in *A Pair of Blue Eyes* (ch. xxxiv).

AT WAKING (p. 177). The woman is probably Tryphena Sparks.

AT A SEASIDE TOWN IN 1869 (p. 178). The town was Weymouth. 'Morgenblätter' = a set of waltzes by Johann Strauss.

THE PHOTOGRAPH (p. 182). Possibly that of Tryphena Sparks.

THOUGHTS OF PHENA (p. 183). The only poem to mention Tryphena Sparks by name. H. said that he wrote the first few lines without knowing that she was at that time dying, but completed the poem after news of her death twelve days later on 17 March 1890. She was H.'s first cousin. In the summer of 1869 they had considered themselves engaged.

THE RECALCITRANTS (p. 184). 'The Recalcitrants' had been an early title for *Jude the Obscure* in which Sue Bridehead is partly based on

Tryphena Sparks. The poem seems to match Sue's resistance to conventional views of the marriage contract.

ON THE DEPARTURE PLATFORM (p. **185**). The woman was Florence Emily Dugdale, who became H.'s second wife.

ALIKE AND UNLIKE (p. **186**). Subtitled in MS – 'She speaks'. The speaker is H.'s first wife. They saw the Great Orme's Head (north Wales) on the way to visit Lord Houghton, Viceroy of Ireland in Dublin (May 1893). The latter's sister (acting as hostess on that occasion) was Mrs Florence Henniker, herself a minor novelist, to whom H. grew attached. Further meetings and a correspondence followed when both returned to England. H. imagines his wife recognizing his feelings on that first occasion.

THE DIVISION (p. **186**). Addressed to Mrs Florence Henniker.

A THUNDERSTORM IN TOWN (p. **187**). The woman was probably Mrs Florence Henniker.

A BROKEN APPOINTMENT (p. **190**). The woman was probably Mrs Florence Henniker.

AFTER THE VISIT (p. **191**). '*F.E.D.*' = Florence Emily Dugdale, who became H.'s second wife.

TO LIZBIE BROWNE (p. **192**). The girl was Elizabeth Bishop, daughter of the Stinsford gamekeeper, the most vividly remembered of H.'s early sweethearts.

AT RUSHY-POND (p. **195**). The pond is on Puddletown Heath, near H.'s birthplace. The girl may have been Tryphena Sparks (born at Puddletown).

TO A MOTHERLESS CHILD (p. **195**). The child was the daughter of Tryphena (Sparks) Gale whom H. visited after Tryphena's death in 1890. Cf. Jude imagining Sue's children: 'Every desired renewal of an existence is debased by being half alloy' (*Jude the Obscure*, Pt. III, ch. viii).

CONCERNING AGNES (p. **196**). Agnes Grove (later Lady Grove, d. Dec. 1926) had been the last woman H. had danced with. This was in the pleasure-grounds laid out by her father Lieutenant-General Augustus Pitt-Rivers on his estate at Rushmore near Salisbury. The occasion was the 'Larmer Tree' sports – named, like the Avenue, after a tree associated with King John's hunting parties.   'Aphrodite' = goddess of love.   'Kalupso' (Calypso) = daughter of the Titan Atlas; she entertained Odysseus for seven years.   'Amphitrite' = goddess of the sea, wife of Poseidon.   'Nine' = the nine Greek muses.

LOUIE (p. **197**). Louisa Harding, one of H.'s early loves, lies buried near H.'s first wife ('the elect one') in Stinsford churchyard.

IN DEATH DIVIDED (p. **197**). The woman addressed was probably Mrs Florence Henniker. See the poem 'The Division'.

THE FIVE STUDENTS (p. **198**). 'dark He' = Horace Moule, H.'s early friend and mentor (suicide 1873); 'fair He' = probably Hooper Tolbort, an early Dorchester friend also helped by Moule (d. 1883); 'dark She' = Tryphena Sparks (d. 1890, though the poem makes hers the second death); 'fair She' = Emma, H.'s first wife (d. 1912).

ON THE ESPLANADE (p. **201**). In 1869 H. was working as an architect in Weymouth. The 'Fate' was the following year's visit to Cornwall where he met Emma.

THE WIND'S PROPHECY (p. **202**). The poem dramatizes H.'s first journey to St Juliot in Cornwall (March 1870), unconscious that Emma Gifford was soon to replace Tryphena Sparks as the loved one.   'Skrymer' = giant in Norse myth.   'pharos' = lighthouse.

'WHEN I SET OUT FOR LYONNESSE' (p. **203**). 'Lyonnesse' = the name in Arthurian romance for Cornwall and drowned land off its coast.

A MAN WAS DRAWING NEAR TO ME (p. **204**). The speaker is Emma. The places mentioned are between Launceston and St Juliot.

DITTY (p. **206**). '(E.L.G.)' = Emma Lavinia Gifford, H.'s first wife.

FETCHING HER (p. **207**). H. addresses himself, lamenting the difference between Emma in her original Cornish setting and in her later home at Max Gate.

A SECOND ATTEMPT (p. **208**). Dated 'About 1900' in MS – hence 'thirty years after' his first meeting with Emma.

LOST LOVE (p. **209**). The speaker is Emma.

LONELY DAYS (p. **210**). The subject is the increasing loneliness and bitterness of Emma's last years at Max Gate. Stanza 2 refers to her earlier life at St Juliot, and stanza 3 to a visit to Plymouth where she was born.

UNDER THE WATERFALL (p. 211). The speaker is Emma, who recorded the incident of the lost drinking-glass in 'Some Recollections'. It had happened on H.'s second visit to St Juliot, August 1870.

THE GOING (p. 213). This is the first of twenty-one poems which H. collected under the general title 'Poems of 1912–13'. Fifteen poems from that group (down to 'Where the Picnic Was') are here included. As a group they carried an epigraph from Virgil's *Aeneid* IV, 23 – '*Veteris vestigia flammae*', the remains of an old fire – and are a response to the death of his first wife on 27 November 1912. Mixing memory and desire and a sense of personal guilt, H. was to write over a hundred poems exploring his sense of loss. 'Beeny Crest' = one of the Cornish cliffs near St Juliot ('beetling' = ramming, crushing).

RAIN ON A GRAVE (p. 216). 'daisies' – Emma's 'Some Recollections' shows that this flower had been a favourite since childhood.

'I FOUND HER OUT THERE' (p. 217). 'Dundagel' = Tintagel, with ruins called 'King Arthur's Castle', which H. had seen on his 1870 visits to Cornwall. 'sunk Lyonnesse' – the drowned land beyond Cornwall's southern coast celebrated in Arthurian legend.

THE HAUNTER (p. 219). Spoken by Emma.

A DREAM OR NO (p. 221). H. was planning a visit to Emma's Cornwall. 'Bos' = Boscastle, into whose harbour runs the Valency River (near St Juliot).

AFTER A JOURNEY (p. 222). H. revisited Cornwall in March 1913. The poem was also influenced by Emma's descriptions of his 1870 visits in 'Some Recollections'. 'Pentargan Bay' is a mile north of Boscastle Harbour, near St Juliot.

AT CASTLE BOTEREL (p. 224). 'Castle Boterel' = H.'s name for Boscastle, near St Juliot.

PLACES (p. 225). H. returned from his Cornish visit via Plymouth, where Emma was born. 'beneaped' = stranded, like a ship at low or 'neap' tide.

THE PHANTOM HORSEWOMAN (p. **226**). Emma had been an accomplished rider. In *Satires of Circumstance* (1914), the 'Poems of 1912–13' had ended with this poem. Three other poems were added in later collections.

WHERE THE PICNIC WAS (p. **227**). The picnic was probably in 1912 (cf. 'last year') and the other two picnickers possibly visitors from London to Max Gate.

'MY SPIRIT WILL NOT HAUNT THE MOUND' (p. **229**). Emma says that her ghost will haunt, not Stinsford Churchyard where she was buried, but the scenes of their courtship in Cornwall.

THE FIGURE IN THE SCENE (p. **232**). H.'s sketch (on Beeny Cliff, August 1870) is now in the County Museum at Dorchester.

THE MARBLE TABLET (p. **233**). The tablet, designed by H., is in St Juliot's Church.

THE SHADOW ON THE STONE (p. **233**). 'the Druid stone' was erected on the lawn at Max Gate (1891), having been unearthed from the garden. Ironically, H. had once found Emma burning his love-letters to her behind the stone.

TEN YEARS SINCE (p. **234**). On the tenth anniversary of Emma's death.

DURING WIND AND RAIN (p. **235**). The scenes were derived from Emma's 'Some Recollections' which describes her childhood homes in Plymouth.

Index of Titles

Abbreviations

HS	*Human Shows* (1925)
LLE	*Late Lyrics and Earlier* (1922)
MV	*Moments of Vision* (1917)
PPP	*Poems of the Past and the Present* (1902)
SC	*Satires of Circumstance* (1914)
TL	*Time's Laughingstocks* (1909)
WP	*Wessex Poems* (1898)
WW	*Winter Words* (1928)

Index of First Lines